TRINITY COLLEGE DUBLIN 1592-1992

TRINITY
400

THE BOLD COLLEGIANS

THE GENEROUS SUPPORT OF AIB BANK
TOWARDS THE PUBLICATION OF THIS BOOK
IS GRATEFULLY ACKNOWLEDGED

THE
BOLD COLLEGIANS

The Development of Sport in
Trinity College, Dublin

Trevor West

At evening when strolling
Down by the college wall,
You'd see the bold collegians
A-playing at the ball . . .

FROM 'THE BONNY BOY',
17TH-CENTURY BALLAD

THE LILLIPUT PRESS
in association with
D·U·C·A·C

First published in 1991 by
THE LILLIPUT PRESS LTD
4 Rosemount Terrace, Arbour Hill,
Dublin 7, Ireland

in association with

Dublin University Central Athletic Club
27 Trinity College, Dublin 2, Ireland

A CIP record for this
title is available from
the British Library.

ISBN 0 946640 80 7

Jacket design by The Graphiconies (Ramaioli)
Set in 10 on 12 Palatino
TEX-generated by the Artech Partnership
and printed in Dublin by
Colour Books of Baldoyle

CONTENTS

Illustrations   vi
The DUCAC Clubs, 1991-92   vii
Honorary Secretaries of DUCAC   viii
Acknowledgements   ix
Abbreviations   x

Introduction   1
1 The College   5
2 The Early Clubs   13
3 The College Races and the Athletic Union   37
4 The Gaelic Athletic Association   53
5 Postwar Revival   59
6 Consolidation   67
7 Expansion   80
8 Current Affairs   98

Appendix 1: Irish Intervarsity Trophies   113
Appendix 2: Riot in 1858   115
Appendix 3: Boat Club Reminiscences   117
Appendix 4: Rules of American Football, 1872   119
Appendix 5: D.U. Laws of Hurley, 1879   120
Appendix 6: Rules of Hurley, 1882   122

References   125
Bibliography   137
Index   143

ILLUSTRATIONS

following page 22

W.E. Thrift
H. Thrift
J.V. Luce and T.T. West
The Foot-Races Committee, 1861-62
Hurdling in College Park
The Football Club, 1866-67
The Football Club, 1869-70
E.J. Watson
Irish Champion Athletic Club poster, 1873

following page 54

The Hurling Club, 1879
G.F. Fitzgerald attempting to fly, 1895
The Boat Club IV, 1873
J.P. Mahaffy, a cartoon
The College Races, 1874
Handball, a cartoon
Hurling, a cartoon
The Lawn Tennis Team, 1886
The Cycling Club with Oliver St J. Gogarty, 1899
The Cricket Club, 1881
The Cricket Club *v.* W.G. Grace's XI, 1903
The River Liffey at Islandbridge
The Hockey XI, 1905-06
Four golfers, including Samuel Beckett
The Trinity and Edinburgh University Ladies' Tennis Teams
Maeve Kyle, 1962
Lacrosse in College Park, 1956
Michael Halliday

following page 86

Jonah Barrington
John Prior, 1974
The Boat Club at Henley, 1981
The Boxing Club with the Christle brothers, 1978
Hugo MacNeill, 1987
Brendan Mullin, 1991

THE DUCAC CLUBS, 1991-92

Aikido

Association Football

Badminton

Basketball

Boat

Boxing

Camogie

Canoe

Croquet

Climbing

Cricket

Cycling

Fencing

Football

Gaelic Football

Golf

Handball

Harriers and Athletics

Hockey

Hurling

Judo

Karate

Lawn Tennis

Orienteering

Olympic Handball

Potholing

Riding

Rifle

Sailing

Squash

Sub-Aqua

Swimming

Table Tennis

Trampolining

Volleyball

Windsurfing

*Where separate men's and women's clubs exist in
a sport, such as rowing, only one club is listed.*

HONORARY SECRETARIES OF DUCAC

1919	J. J. Kelly	1959	J. L. Baxter
1920	L. Smith / I. S. Gamble	1960	C. J. Lea
1921	I. S. Gamble	1961	P. G. R. Heaney
1922-23	F. G. MacManaway	1962	S. S. Newman
1924-25	D. St Clair Mackenzie	1963	M. P. Bagley
1926	T. J. Millin	1964	M. S - M. Hannon
1927-28	J. C. Cherry	1965	C. D. Anderson
1929-30	N. R. Fleming	1966	J. A. Gray
1931	J. W. Craig	1967	J. S. Stubbings
1932-33	R. A. French	1968	A. J. E. O'Sullivan
1934	J. C. Cole	1969	R. McN. Boyd
1935	R. J. O'Neill	1970	R. T. M. Ahern
1936-37	H. A. Dougan	1971	R. M. Spring
1938	W. J. Thompson /	1972	P. R. Coulson
	W. N. R. Millar	1973	A. T. Blackley
1939	J. R. B. McDonald	1974	A. J. McCollum
1940	W. D. Boyle	1975	T. J. O'B. Furlong
1941	P. St G. Anderson	1976	R. G. Booth
1942-43	F. G. Cooke	1977	N. M. Crowley
1944-46	P. R. Oliver	1978	P. J. A. Mullen
1947	A. M. Wiley	1979-80	A. V. P. Hewson
1948-49	R. Blackburn	1981	R. F. Blake
1950	J. V. Grealy	1982	J. S. O'Neill
1951-52	P. N. Ross	1983	E. J. Devlin
1953	P. D. Little /	1984-85	W. H. Kinsman
	G. B. Wheeler	1986	F. T. Burke /
1954	G. B. Wheeler		N. A. de Sousa
1955	J. C. Pearson	1987-89	B. P. J. Cassidy
1956	H. G. Reynolds	1990	A. F. F. Cox
1957-58	G. B. R. Fisher	1991	J. W. R. B. Somerville

ACKNOWLEDGEMENTS

The author wishes to acknowledge the help and encouragement given him in the writing of this book by many friends:

Dr John Andrews, Mr Peter Ashe, Mr Sandy Blackley, Mr Raymond Blake, Mr Marcus Bourke, the late Mr Cyril Boyle, Mr Maurice Bryan, Mr Peter Bunbury, Dr John Byrne, Mr Alister Chisholm, Mr Carson Clarke, the Commodore of the Royal Irish Yacht Club, Mr Jim Cooke, Mr John Cordner, Mr Seán Creedon, Mr Bill Cunningham, Mr Jimmy Davidson, Mr George Dawson, Mr Brendan Dempsey, Mr Kieran Dowd, the late Mrs Elizabeth Duffin, Mr Aidan Duggan, Mr Jim Flynn, Mr Robert Francis, Dr Alastair Gillespie, Mr Oliver Gogarty, Mr Michael Halliday, Mr Tony Hanahoe, Mr Danny Hearn, Mr Niall Hogan, the late Mr Sarsfield Hogan, Dr Richard Holt, Dr Barry Hooper, Dr John Kelly, Mrs Maeve Kyle, Mr Seán Kyle, Mrs Barbara Lomas, Dr John Luce, Dr Bill McCormack, Dr Brendan MacDowell, Dr Brian McGing, Mr Hugo MacNeill, Dr Patrick Meenan, Dr Gerald Morgan, Mr Patrick Moss (Secretary of the Irish Rugby Football Union), Dr Jacques Noël, Mr Ulick O'Connor, the late Dr Raymond Oliver, Mr Liam Ó Muirthile, Dr Tony O'Neill, Mr John Pearson, Dr Murray Power, Mr Francis Quinlan, Mr Peter Read, Mr Terence Read, Mr Daniel Rooney, Mr Bob Russell, Mr Derek Scott (Honorary Secretary of the Irish Cricket Union), Mr Dermot Sherlock, Mr Tony Sparshott, Mr Jack Sweeney, Mr Robin Tamplin, Mr Tommy Ticher, Fr Mark Tierney, Mrs Daphne Tyrrell, Mr John Watterson, Dr William Watts, Dr David Webb, Mr John West, Mr George Wheeler, Dr Cyril White, and Mr Charles Woodhouse.

The author also wishes to thank his colleagues, the directors of athletics in universities around the world, and the staffs of the *Irish Times* Archive, Trinity College Library, and the National Library of Ireland.

ABBREVIATIONS

AAA	Amateur Athletic Association
AAUE	Amateur Athletic Union of Éire
BLE	Bord Lúthchleas na hÉireann
BUSF	British Universities Sports Federation
CUSAI	Council of University Sports Administrators in Ireland
DUBC	Dublin University Boat Club
DUCAC	Dublin University Central Athletic Committee (*since 1960*, Club)
DUCC	Dublin University Cricket Club
DUFC	Dublin University Football Club
DUHC	Dublin University Hockey Club
DURC	Dublin University Rowing Club
FAI	Football Association of Ireland
FISU	Fédération Internationale du Sport Universitaire
FTCD	Fellow of Trinity College, Dublin
GAA	Gaelic Athletic Association
IAAA	Irish Amateur Athletic Association
IAAF	International Amateur Athletic Federation
ICAC	Irish Champion Athletic Club
IFA	Irish Football Association
IRFU	Irish Rugby Football Union
NACAI	National Athletic and Cycling Association of Ireland
NIAAA	Northern Ireland Amateur Athletic Association
NIHE	National Institute for Higher Education
TCD	Trinity College, Dublin
TT	Tourist Trophy
UCC	University College, Cork
UCD	University College, Dublin
UDA	Ulster Defence Association

Introduction

Dublin University Central Athletic Club (DUCAC) is a body composed of students, staff members and graduates that was established by the Board of Trinity College to revive sport in the university after the First World War. Essentially a federation of the college sports clubs, DUCAC has two features that distinguish it among sporting bodies: its records exist almost intact back to its foundation; and, over a span of seventy years, there have been only four chairmen. It was therefore a modest though important task for the fourth of these chairmen to prepare a brief history of DUCAC for the University Quatercentenary in 1991-92. However, material in Trinity College Library referring to bodies which were clearly antecedents of DUCAC, stretching back to the middle of the nineteenth century, suggested that a wider remit be taken. Moreover, Trinity's senior clubs–Cricket, Boat, Football, and Athletics (all more than a century old)–have played central, often dominant, roles in the establishment of their particular sporting disciplines in Ireland.

The origins of these clubs play a prominent part in this book, which is *not* intended to be a history of sport in the university; rather it is on the development of the clubs themselves, and on facilities such as grounds, pavilions, river-bank sites, and sports halls, as well as on the federations, administrative structures and codes of rules established to guide and underpin the clubs, that this work centres.

Dublin University Football Club Foot Races Committee, established in 1857, is the earliest predecessor of DUCAC. The committee evolved in 1872 into the University Athletic Club (a federal association rather than a club *per se*), and ten years later this body became the University Athletic Union. A minute-book of the Foot Races Committee for the period 1866-73 survives, and that of the Athletic Union for 1879-82. There are also frequent references to the activities of these bodies, as well as to the individual clubs (not all of which are complimentary), in the College Register (the Board Minutes).

The Football Club Foot Races Committee, the Athletic Club and the Athletic Union–which was in existence up to the beginning of the First World War–were all federal bodies (the first two informally constituted and the third formally so), containing representatives of the various clubs, and possessing an income out of which they were able to make grants to the clubs. Thus in a real sense they were precursors of DUCAC, giving rise to an unbroken if at times rather wavering line of student-staff-graduate administration of sport in Trinity College.

Similar federations set up to administer sport, with a wide participation and of considerable antiquity, exist in other universities. In Scotland the Edinburgh University Athletic Club dates from 1866,[1] the Glasgow University Athletic Club was founded in 1881,[2] and the Aberdeen University Athletic Association in 1889.[3] Further afield the Athletic Association of the University of Pennsylvania was founded in 1873,[4] the University of Toronto Athletic Association in 1893,[5] and the Adelaide University Sports Association four years later.[6] However, university sport was firmly established long before any of these federations was summoned into being: the first Oxford and Cambridge cricket match was played at Lord's in 1827, and the first boat race between these ancient universities held between Hambleden Lock and Henley Bridge on the River Thames two years later.

Histories of Trinity's four senior clubs have been published. The Football Club, as befits the oldest rugby club in continuous existence, has two such volumes to its credit: a centenary history[7] and a volume of team photographs edited by F. C. Jackson.[8] In 1982 M. H. A. Milne, N. P. Perry, M. E. J. Halliday, M. R. Beamish and E. H. Murray combined to produce a volume to celebrate one-and-a-half centuries of Trinity cricket,[9] while Alan Gilsenan has edited a centenary history of the Harriers and Athletic Club.[10] Trinity College Library contains an extensive collection of records, membership books, minute-books, account books and other documents deposited by the Boat Club, which have been distilled into a history for the Quatercentenary by Raymond Blake.[11] But apart from club records and minute-books, the library's outstanding sporting collection consists of the Watson Papers, deposited in 1981 by the family of H. M. Read, one of Trinity's greatest sportsmen.

Edward J. McCartney Watson, a Dubliner, studied electrical engineering in Cambridge, winning a half-blue in the shot-put in 1895. He then read medicine at Trinity, was university shot-put champion, and became a radiologist in Sir Patrick Dun's Hospital, attached to the university's Medical School. His lifelong interest in sport led him to serve on the Central Athletic Committee and to act as medical adviser and archivist to a number of the clubs, his connection with football, cricket and athletics being particularly strong. The preservation of many of the early records of Trinity sport is in no small measure due to Watson. He married Ina Read, sister of Harry Read, a triple international (football, cricket, and tennis), and died in 1947.

Watson was fascinated by the history of Trinity's older clubs, and many of his papers consist of records of the Football, Cricket and Athletic Clubs culled from newspapers and almanacs. Some of his papers are not connected directly with sport in Trinity; there is, for example, a fascinating scrapbook of the Cambridge University athletic season of 1895 which included a tour of the east coast of the United States. There are also records of the participation of Sir Patrick Dun's in the Dublin Hospitals Cup, a rugby trophy first competed for in 1882.

But the bulk of Watson's papers focuses on the history of the Football Club. He compiled match results, membership lists, and team lists (collating them with the club photographs), going back to the 1850s. In 1928 he decided to publish the fruit of his researches on the history of the Football Club, and his article appeared in 1930 in *The College Pen*; but there were still many questions unanswered, and he had the inspired idea of writing to the surviving members of the early club in an attempt to fill the gaps in his knowledge. Not surprisingly, no survivors were unearthed from the 1850s (they would have had to be ninety years old in 1930), but a number emerged from the next two decades. Among these was John G. Cronyn (whose brother A. P. played on the first Irish team), a member of Dublin University Football Club from 1875 to 1878 who played thereafter for Lansdowne and represented Munster in its first interprovincial. Others were

Alfred Perceval Graves and Arnold Felix Graves, brothers who played football for Trinity in the late 1860s. But it was another student of that era, Charles Burton Barrington (1848-1943), who proved to be the most fertile source of information on the earliest manifestations of rugby in Trinity, and in Ireland.

Barrington came from a distinguished Anglo-Irish family with a seat at Glenstal in Co. Limerick. He succeeded to the family baronetcy in 1890, and became High Sheriff of Limerick. His family had founded Barrington's Hospital in Limerick in 1829; and Barrington's Pier and Barrington's Bridge are other reminders of his family's long connection with the city.[12] He entered Trinity in January 1867, having been educated at St Columba's College in Rathfarnham near Dublin, and at Rugby School; captained the Football Club in 1867-68, 1868-69 and 1869-70; and was to a large extent reponsible for the modernization of the game in Ireland.

Barrington remained fit and vigorous in his later years, driving an ambulance in France during the First World War at the age of sixty-seven. He retained his interest in Trinity football to the end of his life, regularly sending the club captain a congratulatory telegram on the occasion of a notable victory; referring to club members in 1930 as 'my Rugger great-grandchildren'. His only daughter was tragically killed in a republican attack on her car, which was carrying a district inspector of the Auxiliaries when returning from a day's fishing near Newport in Co. Tipperary during the Anglo-Irish conflict in 1921. The Barrington family then moved to England, and Sir Charles offered the family seat to the Free State government as a presidential residence; this offer was not taken up.[13] The house is now a Benedictine priory attached to a school where, as its former owner would have wished, a strong rugby tradition is maintained.

Barrington was eighty-one when he corresponded with Watson, describing incidents that had occurred on and off the field of play some sixty years before. His letters, which are quoted in the text, show that he had lost none of his passion for the game, his exuberant humour, or his *joie de vivre*. They constitute a remarkable record by an equally remarkable man of the early days of football in Trinity College.

1

The College

Man, the distinguished Dutch historian Huizinga reminds us, cannot be totally encapsulated either as *Homo sapiens* (man the thinker) or as *Homo faber* (man the maker), for he is equally *Homo ludens* (man the player).[1] Play, Huizinga suggests, is not a rational activity. Possessed of aesthetic qualities as well as tension and humour, play offers relaxation, rhythm, challenge. It is an embodiment of youth, of strength, of life; above all else, playing must be fun.

Sport, as practised in the university, satisfies Huizinga's criteria. Irrationality is, perhaps too often, the order of the day. While university sport can occasionally attain the sublime, it reaches fair but not too acerbic levels of competition; it is frequently interlaced with humour; it regularly results in true companionship; and its participants have reached that idyllic (perhaps never to be repeated) stage in their adult lives when they do such things essentially for fun.

The University of Dublin, with its sole college, Trinity, was granted its charter by Elizabeth I in 1592. It was established *juxta Dublin*, outside the walls, and somewhat downriver from the medieval city. At the foundation, Dublin contained less than ten thousand inhabitants; as the city grew and the River Liffey was drained, the university found itself on an enclosed 24-acre site right in the heart of the metropolis.

The Elizabethan buildings were modest, and none survives. Trinity's distinguished architecture dates from the Georgian period and is concentrated in the western sector of the campus. Scientific and medical buildings were added in Victoria's reign near the eastern boundary. In the middle lies the College Park, a grassy area of some eight acres that has been used for recreation since it was laid out early in the eighteenth century.

The college's body corporate consists of the Provost, fellows, and scholars. The scholars, as students, take no part in administration, and the college was run by the Provost and seven senior fellows until 1911, when representatives of the junior fellows and of the non-fellow professors were added to the Board. Until 1873, with the abolition of religious tests, fellows had to be members of the Established Church and were normally in holy orders. The challenge to government by seniority would have come sooner than it did had not the tithe system made a country parish more remunerative than a fellowship.

Games were prohibited by the college's early statutes,[2] no doubt because of the violence, gambling and drinking that regularly accompanied them.[3] In 1628 the fellow-commoners complained of a Mr Price 'forbidding them to play at bowls in the orchard'; but Mr Price was in the right, for 'it was showed by Statute they should not play there'.[4]

These edicts forced the more vigorous among the student body to take their exercise without the walls. Outside the college, on the present site of St Andrew's Church, lay the Dublin Bowling Green, described by John Dunton in 1699 as 'perhaps the finest in Europe'.[5] College policy, however, was directed at discouraging the undergraduates from sampling the delights of 'this lewd and debauched town'—a description of seventeenth-century Dublin by Provost Narcissus Marsh.[6] Presumably it was this consideration that led to a change in policy at the end of the century, resulting in the laying-out of a bowling green in 1684[7] and the construction of a fives court ten years later[8] and a real tennis court* in 1741.[9] A map of 1761 shows the bowling green to the east of College Park.[10] The fives court was built at the east end of the Fellows' Garden, probably on a site now occupied by New Square, while the real tennis court, designed by the distinguished architect Richard Cassels, lay near the present Pearse Street boundary, and consisted of a covered rectangular

---

* Real tennis, which is probably of French origin, is played on a court with a strange shape that perhaps derives from monastic cloisters. There are galleries on two sides of the court with sloping roofs, and a net which is not placed in the middle of the court, the service being always taken from the smaller side. The ball is played across the net but may rebound off the walls or the gallery roof. There is now only one court in Ireland, on Lambay Island. The game has been played in Oxford for 500 years and in Cambridge for at least 350. (The author is indebted to Dr J. V. Luce for the references to fives and real tennis.)

court, 85 feet by 25 feet, with galleries along two sides. In 1784 the Board agreed to purchase a field on the northern boundary of College Park to lay out a new bowling green.[11] The Provost of the day, John Hely-Hutchinson, was a keen promoter of riding and fencing as gentlemanly accomplishments for his flock, as well as dancing – hence his nickname 'the Prancer' – and the speaking of foreign languages.

It is not clear that the northern bowling green was ever constructed, and no records exist of the playing of fives, real tennis or bowls in the college in the seventeenth or eighteenth centuries. The real tennis court vanished with the laying out of Great Brunswick Street (now Pearse Street) in the early nineteenth century, and the fives court had disappeared before building started in New Square, while the bowling green was eventually incorporated into College Park.

St Patrick's Well, situated in the Nassau Street wall near the Dawson Street gate, was once the most celebrated holy well in Dublin and the resort of pilgrims from all over Ireland. In 1688 a Danish *Thingmote*, or council mound, one hundred yards to the west of the college was removed and the soil deposited on St Patrick's Well Lane, the forerunner of Nassau Street, leading to the considerable difference in level with the College Park.

On 8 June 1722 a number of young trees were cut down in the area of the park, a student being expelled for the offence. College Park was then formally laid out and its perimeter planted with elm and plane trees. In the same year a wall was built on the eastern boundary of the park with a lodge for a porter.[12] The park was then intersected by a broad ditch known as the 'ha-ha', which ran diagonally from the old Printing House to the site of the present Pavilion.* Tradition has it that in places it was twenty feet wide and that it was used by students to test their skill at the long jump. In Lever's novel *Charles O'Malley* a porter is immersed in the ha-ha, from which he emerges 'dripping with duck-weed, like an insane river-god'.[13] The park was drained in 1813,[14] and further drainage was carried out in the 1850s.[15] The ha-ha was ultimately filled in, and the water table is maintained at the correct level by continuous pumping.

* In an exceptionally dry summer the line of a drain appears running along the course of the 'ha-ha' diagonally across the grass in New Square, continuing across the cricket ground to the north-western corner of the Pavilion.

Riot and disorder were common in the college during the early eighteenth century, when Jacobite feeling was still evident among the student body, and fighting between town and gown was a feature of Dublin life. In 1734 an unpopular junior fellow, Ford, was shot through a window of his rooms in the Rubrics, a range of red-brick residential housing in the middle of the college. Five students who were sent down were later acquitted of murder by the Court of Commission;[16] others, including the poet Oliver Goldsmith, were publicly censured by the Board. Nearing the end of the century these outbursts greatly diminished; moreover, the gaming, drinking and duelling for which the Irish gentry were notorious were going out of fashion, and youthful energies were redirected into more civilized channels.

From its foundation members of the college, both staff and students, would in the natural course of things have taken part in athletic activities such as running, jumping, throwing, and wrestling, in archery[17] and gunnery, in aquatic sports, and in equestrian pursuits. Organized games, their codification and the formation of sports clubs are nineteenth-century phenomena, which germinated in the English public schools, took root in the ancient universities, and then spread rapidly throughout urban Britain.

By 1850 the average age at entrance had risen to its present level; one-tenth of the students were Catholics (a smaller percentage were Dissenters); and, although the university always contained a leaven of distinguished nationalists, and student opinion was at times decidedly radical, the college was a bastion of unionism from the Act of Union in 1800 until the break with the United Kingdom in 1922. Prohibition by the hierarchy, promulgated originally in 1875, ensured that the number of Catholic students in the twentieth century grew unnaturally slowly, and it was 1970 before Catholics made up half the student body. Women were admitted to the college in 1904.

Apart from equestrian and canine pursuits and such pastimes as shooting and fishing, the traditional Irish sports are probably athletics, hurling, handball, fighting (boxing and wrestling), football, and bowling. Road bowling (propelling a lead ball between two marks along a road in the least number of 'bowls') is still common in the counties of Cork and Armagh. In 1813 Provost Elrington proposed to lattice the east windows of the dining hall to provide an area for ball-players.[18] Presumably it was the activities of student handballers that persuaded the Board in 1831 to reimburse a resident of nearby Great Brunswick Street the handsome sum of £10 17s 6d for windows broken by ball-players.[19] In 1849 a student petition for the erection of ball-courts* evoked the response that 'the Board did not think it expedient at present to take the subject into consideration'.[20] Continued pressure paid off, for by 1862 the Board had approved the rules drawn up for the management of a racket court,† and had given a grant of £100 towards its construction 'in the north-east angle of the College Park'.[21]

In 1833 the Board received a memorial from the student body concerning the erection of a gymnasium.[22] Nothing, however, was done, and when the request was renewed six years later it was peremptorily rejected.[23] By 1868 the climate had changed, but an obstacle was the debt outstanding on the racket court. The memorialists had by this time acquired a determined and resourceful tribune in the ubiquitous sportsman and fellow, Anthony Traill; and the following agreement was eventually hammered out between the Board and the Gymnasium Committee:

1. That the debt at present due from the Racket Court Committee be paid off and that a further sum of £200 be contributed by parties proposing to erect the gymnasium.
2. That the erection of the gymnasium be conducted under the direction of the Bursar in conjunction with the subscribers.
3. That the rules of the gymnasium be approved by the Board and be not altered without their consent.[24]

On these terms the Board agreed to advance £1000 towards the cost of the gymnasium at three and a half per cent, the interest to be a first charge on admission fees to be paid by the users.[25] The gymnasium was constructed alongside the racket court to the north-east of College Park. Shortly after it was completed, in 1872, an exhibition was held before a large crowd, featuring vaulting, boxing, fencing, Indian clubs, the horizontal bar, the trapeze, and rope and pole climbing.[26]

In the early years of the nineteenth century only the southern

---

* The University Rowing Club constructed a ball-alley in its headquarters at Ringsend in 1845. Trinity handballers now play in the handball courts in the GAA headquarters at Croke Park.

† Rackets was the forerunner of squash, played on a larger court with a harder ball.

9

of the two fields that now make up the College Park was used, informally, for cricket, hurling, football, and various types of athletics. The Board in 1842 directed that a proper cricket pitch be laid out;[27] and when some ten years later football came to be played in an organized way, a piece of ground known as the 'swamp' was the original pitch. This was a narrow strip lying between the trees along the Nassau Street railings and the cricket square, which was not then as wide as it is at present. Hurling was probably played at either end of the cricket square, but the arrangement *vis-à-vis* cricket and football was unsatisfactory, for the swamp was too narrow and too wet for football; and as a result of the footballers' depredations the outfield, at the beginning of each cricket season, needed major repairs.

As games developed and as the numbers of participants and clubs increased, the need for a second field became more pressing, leading to approaches to the Board for permission to use what was known as the Wilderness, the tract of land to the north of what is now the Broadwalk through the College Park. 'It was occupied', wrote R.M. Gwynn, a member of one of Trinity's great sporting and academic families, 'by a scanty wood of meagre hawthorns and poplars. The surface was covered with a thin coating of ill-nourished grass, barely hiding the ashes, cinders and broken crockery which had been dumped there at some period when it had been the receptacle for College refuse.'[28]

Attempts to persuade the Board to sanction the use of the Wilderness as a playing-field were regularly rebuffed until the forenoon of 3 November 1899, when providence finally intervened. A fierce but apparently localized hurricane, accompanied by a thick mist, struck the centre of Dublin. A cab in a funeral procession in Great Brunswick Street on the northern boundary of the college was overturned; a portion of the granite coping on the Museum Building overlooking College Park was blown off, and the iron railing adjoining the building was twisted and bent.[29] Only a few of the surrounding trees were felled, but the Wilderness was flattened. A fortnight later the Board considered an application by the Hockey Club;[30] but a joint request from the Cricket and Football Clubs, in favour of the latter, carried the day, and the Bursar was directed to have the Wilderness cleared and levelled.[31] The playing surface was initially scarred with the debris of past generations, and for years, as if to spite the efforts

10

of the Trinity pack, crocuses continued to flourish along one of the twenty-fives in an astonishingly obdurate fashion. To this day the pitch possesses little depth of sod; a compensating factor is the exceptional drying quality of the ground, which with a stiff breeze and sufficient grass cover can appear saturated at breakfast but then have fully dried out by lunchtime.

Ball games can be divided into two main categories, depending on the size of the ball. Perhaps small-ball games have a common origin; the striking resemblance between the modern Irish hurling stick and the ancient English cricket bat, linked to the fact that the early wicket was little more than a miniature goal, indicates a connection between traditional sports in the two islands. In Ireland hurling and football traditionally were parish games played perhaps each year on certain feast days, with few restrictions on the length of the contest, the number of participants, or the extent of the playing area. Wrestling and fighting were part and parcel of these games; and the fact that they were often illegal, in Ireland as elsewhere, served only to increase their popularity.

Traces of these parish games survive in Britain, if not in Ireland. At St Columb Major in Cornwall two annual games, significantly called hurling, in which a silver-covered ball is hurled with the hand by teams consisting of town-dwellers and countrymen, are played on Feast Monday and Shrove Tuesday.[32] (A tradition of Cornish hurling goes back for hundreds of years.) Similar games are still played at Jedburgh on the Scottish border,[33] and at Kirkwall in Orkney.[34] Two distinct forms of hurling seem to have been common in Ireland in the pre-Victorian era: northerners used a stick with a slender boss, resembling the modern shinty stick or hockey stick, while in the south the boss was thicker, as in present-day hurling.

These games were predominantly rural pastimes, and in the Ireland of the nineteenth century rural life, for social, political and economic reasons, had gone into a steep decline. England in Victoria's reign was progressive, prosperous, and open to the great experiments of administration and reform. In Ireland the Act of Union was never supplemented with the requisite governmental energy or initiative; measures that were appropriate in one country were quite inappropriate in the other; industrialization had taken hold only in the north-eastern corner of the island;

and in the 1840s these weaknesses were remorselessly exposed by the Famine.

However, it was precisely at this time that games came to be codified in Britain. Furthermore, because of the building of the railways and the paucity of Irish schooling, the numbers of men (mainly of Irish birth) attending Trinity who had been educated at English public schools increased significantly in mid-century.[*] Trinity, and Dublin, were far less affected by the Famine than were the rural south and west. The university was in fact just embarking on what later came to be referred to as its golden age. Mathematicians such as Hamilton, Salmon, and Fitzgerald, historians of the calibre of Bury and Lecky, and men of letters as distinguished as Mahaffy and his protégé Wilde (who objected to cricket as its postures were 'indecent') were to ensure that Trinity's reputation never stood higher.

The students springing from the gentry, the clergy and the professional classes were less demoralized than their fellow-citizens by the Act of Union or by the Famine.[†] English-educated public school men, fortified by the sporting tradition of the Irish countryside, would have brought back with them the self-confidence that was such a hallmark of the Victorian era; they must also have been aware of, and some of them would have participated in, that process of codification and organization of games spearheaded by the public schools, then rapidly shedding their Dickensian characteristics. The coming of the railways had improved communication internally and between the two islands. Sporting journals reporting in detail on cricket, football, athletics and rowing (besides their regular coverage of the turf) were another phenomenon of the nineteenth century. Along with its knowledge of Irish sports and pastimes, the Trinity community had a clear awareness of, as well as a deep interest in, the developments taking place across the water.

[*] In 1885 it was estimated that at least one thousand Irish boys were being educated in English public schools.[35]

[†] See appendix 2.

2

The Early Clubs

THE CRICKET CLUB

Cricket was introduced to Ireland from England; indeed it is the only Irish sport that can be accurately referred to as a 'garrison game', for cricket clubs sprang up in remarkable profusion around the middle of the nineteenth century in the vicinity of army barracks or on the estates of the gentry. The first recorded cricket match in Ireland took place in the Phoenix Park in 1792, for a wager of five hundred guineas, between the Garrison and 'All Ireland'. The future Duke of Wellington,* who was then aide-de-camp to the Lord Lieutenant, is reputed to have participated on the Irish side.[1]

Cricket was played in Trinity early in the nineteenth century. A ballad written about 1830, praising teams from Garbally, Co. Galway, and Norelands, Co. Kilkenny, refers to cricketers in the college:

> A club was formed in Garbally
> The West of Ireland troublin'
> Who said they would beat all the world
> Three years ago in Dublin.
> They swore the Court and Garrison
> Townspeople and Collegians
> Could not stand in comparison
> With eleven of their Galwegians.[2]

Lawrence's *Handbook of Cricket in Ireland* (1866) dates the university club's foundation as 1835;[3] and it was clearly in existence when the Board took the formal decision to lay out a cricket pitch in the College Park in 1842.[4] Phoenix CC had been founded

---

* The duke's father, the Earl of Mornington, was a Trinity graduate and the first holder of the chair of music in the university. The playing of games, in particular of cricket and fives, became a feature of British army life in the 1840s with Wellington as commander-in-chief.

five years before, and Leinster CC, the third of the original 'big three', ten years after the university club. Records of matches survive from 1845: the University *v*. Phoenix (home and away), and the Graduates and Undergraduates of Trinity College *v*. Rest of the World (the World's innings totalled 21!),[5] as well as games against the military. By mid-century, thanks to the exertions of the gentry and of the garrison, cricket had spread to the most unlikely parts of rural Ireland, as well as gaining a foothold in the larger towns.

Three fellows – Anthony Traill, John Pentland Mahaffy, and George Francis Fitzgerald – played dominant roles in the nurturing of Trinity sport in the nineteenth century. Traill and Mahaffy were future Provosts (Fitzgerald was cut down in his prime at the age of forty-nine), while Mahaffy and Fitzgerald bestrode the academic world. Totally diverse in character, each was a passionate advocate of causes in which he believed. Joined together, as they often were in sporting matters, they became a formidable, often irresistible, trio, whose enthusiasm contributed greatly to the authorities' benevolent view of the college clubs in the latter part of the nineteenth century.

Traill, a blunt Ulsterman from Ballycastle, Co. Antrim, captained the Cricket and Football Clubs, was an enthusiastic mountaineer,* and fourteen times rackets champion: the senior by twelve years, he beat Fitzgerald in a celebrated rackets final in 1880, after losing the first set.[6] Having obtained moderatorships in mathematics and experimental science, he proceeded to doctorates of medicine and of laws, and, as a layman, was a powerful figure in the General Synod, the ruling body of the Church of Ireland after its disestablishment in 1869.

Mahaffy, a better cricketer than Traill, took holy orders, describing himself as 'a clergyman, but not in any offensive sense of the term'. He wrote with authority on German philosophy, Greek social life, Greek papyri (discovered in Egypt), and the college silver; he was a snob, and was the driving force behind the Irish Georgian Society, founded in 1908 to remedy the decay that already blighted Ireland's eighteenth-century architecture. No mean bat (as well as a fine angler and a first-class shot), he

---

* Traill lectured so often, with lantern-slides, on an expedition he had made to the American West that the Rocky Mountains, according to Mahaffy, were worn out by Traill's constant climbing!

was an excellent bowler who, unlike most practitioners of his art, was more effective when the ball was wet. In 1871 he bowled out a United South of England Eleven, captained by G. F. Grace, and in the following year repeated the feat against an All-England Eleven (the university regularly put out a team of eighteen or twenty-two players against such formidable opposition). In cricketing circles he was known as 'the General'!

On one occasion the well-known Philadelphian cricketer J. B. King, visiting College Park and not knowing Mahaffy, found him demonstrating his batting skills to admiring mortals around the cricket net. Having assessed the scene, King addressed Mahaffy: 'Sir, if I were bowling to you, I would require only one fieldsman to take your wicket.' 'Indeed,' replied the irritated Mahaffy, 'and where would you place him?' 'Twenty yards behind the stumps,' King replied, 'to pick up the bails.' On another occasion a student, Wilkinson, with a companion, was brought by the Junior Dean before Provost Traill on a disciplinary matter, Mahaffy being in attendance. The Junior Dean's voice was barely audible. 'What's he saying? What's he saying?' barked the Provost. 'He's trying to tell you, Mr Provost, that these students were conducting an iconoclastic crusade in Front Square.' Traill rounded on Wilkinson's friend. 'You don't work and you take no part in college sport. Wilkinson at least passes his examinations and plays for the university at cricket and soccer. You are fined two pounds.'

Mahaffy—who graduated in 1859, became a fellow in 1864, and was made professor of ancient history in 1869—articulated an Anglo-Irish philosophy of sport that, he felt, applied to Trinity in the 1870s.[*] He was then at the height of his intellectual and cricketing prowess, and his ideas are of interest as, at the time, sporting success was rivalling academic achievement in the English public schools and at Oxford and Cambridge.[7] The relative poverty of Trinity men, he argued, combined with the consequent necessity to graduate and find employment, prevented an undue emphasis being placed on sport by the students.[8] The field sports of hunting, shooting and fishing were moreover the prerogative of every Irishman, and not simply

[*] A fine philosophical chapter, necessarily confined to a single sport, is to be found in A. A. Luce's *Fishing and Thinking* (London 1959; second edition, Shrewsbury 1990).

reserved for the rich as they were across the water. They gave Irish country gentlemen, he believed, 'an inestimable advantage over the city athlete whose special training for a particular event has a necessary tendency to lower him to a professional'.[9] Although there had been some specialization in cricket and rowing, 'men do not as a rule train hard in the clubs, and treat games as a recreation and not as the main object of life . . . As yet the best oar and best bat is not a great man in Trinity College, he is not thought superior to the best mathematician or classical scholar.'[10]

George Francis Fitzgerald, the third of the trio, was an outstanding mathematical physicist and the leading advocate of scientific and technical education in Ireland. The Fitzgerald-Lorentz contraction in relativity theory is jointly attributed to him. He was an enthusiastic oarsman, a hurler, and a champion pole-vaulter, and in 1895 attempted to fly, descending from a ramp erected against the Pavilion in the College Park. Despite the efforts of numerous enthusiastic students to provide the airman and his quixotic craft with sufficient momentum, the flight was not a success.* Fitzgerald removed his jacket, as illustration 11 shows, but throughout the experiment, as befitted a fellow, he retained his top hat![11]

Trinity cricket benefited from the two extraordinary families of Hone and Gwynn, whose talents extended well beyond the sports field to literature and painting, to scholarship and the Church. Their schooldays were spent at St Columba's College in the foothills of the Dublin Mountains, a school with a strong cricketing tradition. Five of the Hones played cricket for the university, and one, Leland, has the distinction of being the only Irish-bred cricketer to play in a test match in Australia (with Lord Harris's team of 1879). Four Gwynns were notable cricketers, several were distinguished rugby men, and one, E. J., became Provost. Lucius Gwynn, who was an Irish threequarter, was elected to fellowship in 1896; sadly, the date of the fellowship examination clashed with a test match against Australia at Old Trafford for which he had been selected. Before his tragically early death from tuberculosis at the age of twenty-nine, he put

---

* Fitzgerald's craft, a Lilienthal glider, resembled a modern hang-glider. The attempt attracted a considerable crowd of spectators, an irreverent onlooker shouting through the Nassau Street railings, 'Look out, professor, there's bird lime in the park!'

on 133 with Oxford University's greatest all-round sportsman, C. B. Fry, for the Gentlemen against the Players at the Oval in 1895, making 80 before being run out. He played for possibly the strongest DUCC eleven, that of 1893, which defeated Oxford in College Park, and then on tour in England defeated Leicestershire and Warwickshire (dismissed for 15 in their second innings) and drew with Essex.

David Trotter, from Summerhill, Co. Meath, was another prolific scorer in the same era. A poor fielder, he was a fine bat, so impressing W. G. Grace on one of the Doctor's frequent visits to Ireland that he was selected to play for the North against the South at Lord's in 1877. Trotter made 9 and 33 for the North, but the match was dominated by Grace's 261 for the opposition. Arthur Samuels, who graduated in 1848, learned his cricket at the Kingstown School, which was then renowned for having the best hurley team in Ireland![12] An underarm bowler, Samuels was one of the most prolific wicket-takers of his day. The outstanding fast bowlers produced by the club were C. L. Johnson, who later played for South Africa, and Horace Hamilton, who generated great pace off a short run-up. While on an Irish tour of North America in 1879, Hamilton set a Canadian record for the pole vault of 10 feet 1 inch.

On one of W. G. Grace's visits to College Park, J. M. Meldon, the university captain, tossed the coin for choice of innings. 'Woman,' called the Doctor; the coin came down tails; and Meldon, about to declare his preference, was pre-empted by Grace's announcement, 'We'll bat.' Somewhat overawed by the occasion, Meldon returned to the Pavilion to inform his disgruntled eleven that although he believed he had won the toss he was obliged to lead them into the field. The coin, with Victoria's head on one side, had Britannia on the other: the Doctor had shrewdly placed an each-way bet!

In 1878 W. G. Grace presided over a discussion on field sports held in conjunction with the Dublin meeting of the British Association for the Advancement of Science. Mahaffy was vice-chairman. E. M. Grace presented a paper entitled 'The Relative Merits of Curvilinear and Rectilinear Bowling', his brother G. F. Grace also spoke, and W. G. gave a short address in which he praised Irish batting but criticized the lack of application of the native bowlers. The great fault of Irish cricket, he averred, lay in its 'flourish'.[13]

The game of cricket was already highly formalized before it reached Ireland, and, unlike other codes, it was not to be expected that the formation of the university club would have any dramatic effect on the structure of the game. An attempt in 1884 to form an Irish Cricket Union came to nothing when the university and Phoenix refused to join since the proposed constitution gave the same rights to 'major' as to 'minor' clubs.[14] (The Irish Cricket Union was eventually formed only in 1923.) When the former 'swamp' had been resodded in 1904 (with a grant from the Board of £30[15]) the cricket ground, with its city centre location, became even more suitable for major contests, and representative fixtures were regularly staged in the College Park.

THE BOAT CLUB

The convoluted origins of the Boat Club date back to 2 September 1836, when the Pembroke Club (not to be confused with the Pembroke Rowing Club, which came later and had little connection with the university) held its inaugural meeting–chaired by a member of the Hone family–at Radley's Hotel in College Green.[16] The Pembroke Club, which rowed in the Earl of Pembroke's estate at Ringsend near the mouth of the Liffey, consisted mainly of undergraduates but was not confined to them. An early resolution, capturing the spirit of university rowing, decreed: 'That any member marrying shall forfeit a dozen of champagne to the club to be drunk by the members at such time and place as shall be agreed by them.'[17]

Vestiges of two earlier clubs (the Dublin and the Liffey Rowing Clubs) survive, but no records; thus Trinity, tracing its lineage to the formation of Pembroke, is recognized as the senior Irish rowing club. Within two years of its inception the club had over one hundred members, and in 1839 it sent a four to compete in Liverpool. In 1840 the club held the first regatta of any consequence in Ireland at Ringsend, but in 1843 the University Rowing Club was founded by undergraduates (many of whom were members of Pembroke) who wanted a club strictly confined to university men. The next annual report of the Pembroke Club complains that 'the past year was disadvantageous to the interests of the Pembroke Club owing to the formation of a new boat club ... '[18] The minutes of the Pembroke annual general meeting of 1847 indicate that club strength was already affected by the 'anticipation of coming distress'–foreshadowing the Famine–and the committee was empowered to explore means of remedying the situation.[19] Affairs did not remain for long in this unhappy state, for in that same year the University Rowing Club and Pembroke joined forces to form the Dublin University Rowing Club. The new club was to be confined mainly to university men, but provision was made for the election of associate members.

To some extent the merger must have been a shotgun marriage between oarsmen who sought a pure university club and those who wished for wider representation. This problem simmered on, boiling over in 1867 with mass resignations from DURC and the formation of the Dublin University Boat Club. These resignations crystallized around the blackballing of certain Catholic applicants for membership–the only occasion on which sectarianism seems to have corroded Trinity sport;[20] but another bone of contention was a proposal to increase the number of non-university members by one-third.[21] An acerbic letter of resignation arrived from William Traill (Anthony's brother), in which he foresaw no hope of reconciliation, emphasizing his determination to found 'a new *Rowing* club on purely University principles'.[22] The rivalry between the two university clubs, in which no quarter was asked or given, dominated Irish rowing in the latter half of the nineteenth century, and Trinity crews regularly carried off the top prizes in Ireland and indeed at Henley.

Rowing in the earlier part of the century was more primitive than the sophisticated sport we know today. The craft were different, and races took place mainly in estuaries, or sometimes in the open sea. The first Trinity crews rowed near the confluence of the Rivers Liffey and Dodder, in conditions rendered unpleasant by the flotsam of a busy harbour. Difficult conditions led to frequent fouling, and the early regattas, with their differing rules, were often the scenes of acrimonious dispute. The Boat Club played a leading part in the adoption of a uniform set of Irish regatta rules, based on those in use at Henley and accepted by the rowing clubs at Oxford and Cambridge. With the advent of more specialized boats after 1870, regattas gradually moved upriver, and the links between rowing and sailing clubs were broken.*

The junior Trinity club was perhaps the more successful of the two, and under its veteran coach Tom Grant introduced a revolutionary and highly effective style involving a long, slow pull that became celebrated as the 'Boat Club stroke'. At the same period, to obtain greater control prior to the introduction of the sliding seat, Rowing Club crews fitted their trousers with leather, greased their thwarts, and slid on them! The Rowing Club seems to have been favoured by the Board, which in 1881 gave it permission to use the university coat of arms;[24] but the bizarre division continued, and the editorials of the *Irish Sportsman* constantly urged that a Trinity crew be added to those of Oxford and Cambridge for the boat race. Oxford and Cambridge recognized Dublin degrees, argued the *Sportsman*, and similar recognition should be offered to Trinity oarsmen. Had such an invitation been extended, it would have forced the two Trinity clubs to select a composite crew. Nothing came of this too transparent ploy, however, and the split remained.†

In 1883 the Boat Club proposed the formation of a federation for Irish rowing, with the following objects:

1. To maintain the standard of amateur oarsmanship as recognized by the rowing clubs of the United Kingdom;
2. To associate members of Irish amateur rowing clubs for the purpose of forming crews to compete against non-Irish crews when required;
3. To draw up a code of general rules according to which all Irish regattas may be conducted.[25]

The invitation was sent initially to clubs based in Ringsend – the Commercial, Dolphin, University, Neptune and Pembroke Rowing Clubs – and won unanimous acceptance in this quarter.

It is remarkable that with such influential support the proposal should have got no further. The scheme foundered on the vexed question of amateurism, which, with the explosive increase in the numbers of organized sports and their participants, was surfacing to plague the administrators in many codes. This problem was more acute in urban Britain, and there its resolution was to have a devastating effect. In Irish sports – such as athletics or

* The Royal St George Yacht Club – which has strong links with the university Sailing Club – evolved from the Kingstown Yacht Club, formed by members of Pembroke in 1838.[23]

† Unsuccessful attempts were also made to have the university represented by a composite crew at Henley.

rowing—where valuable prizes were on offer and where a practice of betting had emerged among the spectators, professionalism arose as an inevitable consequence. Amateur championships were then introduced, with rules outlawing professionals; but since the administrators were drawn from the leisured classes, a tendency emerged not just to equate professionalism with money payments but also, mistakenly, to assume that the amateur must be a gentleman. Thus artisans, mechanics and the labouring class (including often the lower ranks of the police or army) were excluded from participation in amateur competitions, while university students, as gentlemen, automatically possessed amateur status. The Boat Club's proposals were, on these grounds, looked at unfavourably by the Belfast rowing clubs, and, as the scheme excluded artisans and mechanics, they turned it down.[26]*

At last, in 1898, just as the early dominance of the two university clubs came under challenge, the patience and diplomacy of a former Boat Club captain, W. G. Towers, together with the support of a number of influential figures in college, carried the day, and the clubs were merged. The carrot was the opportunity of moving from Ringsend to a desirable reach of the Liffey at Islandbridge. Difficulties over the name ('Dublin University Boat Club' was felt to be more in tune with the times) and the colours (the black and white of the Rowing Club combined with the college arms on a shield of Boat Club blue) were ironed out by Towers and two fellows, Fitzgerald and John Kells Ingram, professor of oratory and of English literature, better known as author of the patriotic poem 'Who Fears to Speak of Ninety-Eight?' Describing a final event at the old headquarters, a *T.C.D.* correspondent wrote that 7 May 1898 was 'a typical Ringsend day. Rain was falling in torrents; the Dodder appeared in its most uninviting aspect, and the thoughts of everyone turned in anticipation and hope to the approaching migration to new quarters far removed from the mud and chemical works'.[27]

The river at Islandbridge was straightened, with help from the Board; and a grandstand (since removed), boathouse and enclosure were built, so that by 1902 splendid facilities existed at the new club some miles upstream from the old site in Ringsend. Apart from a small subvention from college the

* The Irish Amateur Rowing Union was formed in 1899.

costs of £4,000 were covered by debentures and a mortgage, placing a severe strain on the club's finances. Although the Board gave further support after the First World War, it was 1939 before these obligations were taken on in full, and the Islandbridge site and premises passed into the college's hands.[*]

THE FOOTBALL CLUB

Football, which may have come to Ireland from Britain, was originally a peasant pastime based on the parish or village. It was unregulated and violent, and fatal accidents occurred during matches with alarming frequency.[28] One challenge between neighbouring villages in Co. Derry read, 'for the Late Sleepers to come over on [a certain Sunday] and kick the Early Risers'.[29] The Statutes of Galway (1527) forbade hurling and other sports 'except alone football with the grate ball'.[30] Literary references indicate that football was played in north Co. Dublin in the late seventeenth century. The poet Mathew Concanen, writing in 1720 to celebrate the victory of his native village, Swords, over neighbouring Lusk, reveals that the ball was made of oxhide 'stuffed with the finest hay'; the goals consisted of boughs of sallywood bent into a bow; the ball could be caught and kicked in the air, kicked and rushed along the ground, or carried; and tripping and wrestling, while not strictly legal, yet fell within the spirit of the game.[31] In some parts of the country this game was known by its Irish name of *caid*.[32]

As local matches so often resulted in riot and disorder, the game was regularly declared illegal (Edward II banned football in London in 1314!). Not, however, until Sir Robert Peel organized his police force in England in 1829 was the law regularly enforced; the peelers then cracked down on the undisciplined brand of football prevalent in England, just as a more disciplined code, or codes, had begun to develop in the public schools.

Although William Webb Ellis[†] (who, in 1823, caught the ball and ran with it in a game at Rugby School) is regarded as the progenitor of modern rugby, the spread of the game owes more to

[*] A delightful account by M. P. Leahy of Boat Club activities after the merger is included in appendix 3.

[†] In 1827 Ellis played in the first varsity cricket match for Oxford *v.* Cambridge at Lord's.

W.E. Thrift FTCD*, 1919-37.*   *H. Thrift* FTCD*, 1937-56.*

J.V. Luce FTCD*, 1956-76 and T.T. West* FTCD*, 1976 to date, rival captains in the Fellows* v. *Scholars cricket match in 1960. (Courtesy* The Irish Times*)*

The Foot-Races' Committee 1861-62, with Anthony Traill on extreme right.
(Courtesy TCD Physics Department)

An early photograph of hurdling in College Park, probably taken by John Joly FTCD.
(Courtesy TCD Physics Department)

The Football Club, 1866-67, with C.B. Barrington second from left and R.M. Wall extreme right.

The Football Club, 1869-70, captained by C.B. Barrington, with a gold shamrock emblazoned in his cap.

WATSON, CAMBRIDGE, SHOT-PUTTER.

E.J. Watson, Cambridge shot-putter and Trinity archivist. (Courtesy TCD Library)

Irish Champion Athletic Club poster of the 1873 meeting in the College Park.

Thomas Arnold, the celebrated though controversial headmaster of the school from 1828 to 1842. There is little evidence that Arnold himself was interested in football, although he plays the role of benevolent spectator in the account of the famous Bigside match in *Tom Brown's Schooldays;*[33] but this account is based on an original written by W. D. Arnold, son of the headmaster.[34] In any case Arnold would have been shrewd enough to discern the advantages of organized sports, such as cricket and football, compared with the drinking, bullying, gambling and poaching that were standard diversions in the public schools of his day.*

Many of Arnold's protégés obtained headmasterships, and his influence on the public school system was such that the code of football then practised at Rugby was implanted in schools such as Cheltenham, Marlborough, and Rossall. The style of education attributed to Arnold was based on Christian values, character building, a system of accountability for boys and masters, and Plato's Hellenic ideal of *mens sana in corpore sano;* as this became the model for the Victorian public school, so the rugby gospel spread through those who had served under him.[†] Eton, Charterhouse and Westminster, however, practised another code in which handling was not permitted, leading to the development of association football or soccer.

Football in Trinity certainly pre-dates the foundation of the Football Club in 1854. A poem of Edward Lysaght's, published in 1811, is evidence that football was played in the College Park regularly in the 1780s:

> Dear C–lf–ld, play football no more, I entreat,
> The amusement's too vulgar, fatiguing and rough;
> Pursue the same conduct you've followed of late,
> And I warrant, ere long, you'll get kicking enough.[36]

The poem was published with an accompanying footnote:

At the time when Ned Lysaght was in Trinity College [*c.* 1780] the fellow-commoners considered themselves superior beings to the pensioners;

---

* Significantly, there was no mention of football when Tom Brown went up to Oxford, only rowing, cricket, real tennis, and boxing.[35]

† T.H. Smith, from Co. Monaghan, who entered Trinity in 1846 and later taught in Australia, served with two former pupils of Rugby School on the committee of the Melbourne Cricket Club which in 1859 drew up Australian Rules. American intercollegiate football developed in the 1860s. A set of rules for American football taken from the *Irish Sportsman* in 1872, 'differing somewhat in rules from that played here,' is given in appendix 4.

and of course they were above taking any part in the amusement of football which was then played every evening in the College Park.* It so happened that a pensioner whose name was C–lf–ld, had been vain enough to associate entirely with fellow-commoners, and, of course, never deigned to play at football, until one evening when he accidentally condescended to do so; scarcely had he made the attempt, when some of his fellow students (pensioners) indignant at his past folly, soon tripped up his heels, to the no small gratification of the whole assemblage then present, but to the mortification of C–lf–ld and his companions.

The first formal record of the university club, indicating that it had been in existence for at least a year, appears under the heading 'Trinity College' in the *Daily Express* of 1 December 1855:

> FOOT BALL.–A match will be played in the College Park today (Saturday) between original and new members of the club. Play to commence at two o'clock College time.†

For a number of years afterwards, all fixtures were internecine struggles between Internals and Externals, Fair Hair and Dark Hair, Sophisters and the Field, the Football Club and the Boat Club, Cheltenham boys‡ or Royal Schools§ versus the Rest, or Graduates and Senior Sophisters versus the Minor Classes. Football in Trinity also clearly pre-dates any distinctions between the Rugby, Association and (much later) Gaelic codes. The first external fixture took place against Wanderers– possibly a team consisting of former DUFC members–in 1860 (the well-known Dublin club of that name was not founded until 1870). DUFC pioneered the handling game in Ireland. The *Irish Times* of 28 October 1867 records that in three matches against the military,

although the University out of courtesy to the strangers, at first played contrary to custom by the Eton rules, they succeeded in holding their own in one of the first two matches, and were only beaten after a close

---

* Ordinary (middle-class) students were 'pensioners'. 'Fellow-commoners' were sons of the gentry who paid extra for certain privileges. A third, more privileged category of student was *filius nobilis*.

† To ensure prompt attendance at lectures, college time was fifteen minutes behind Dublin time!

‡ Of the thirty-six members of the club who matriculated before 1856, sixteen had been educated at Cheltenham, ten at Rugby, nine at Irish schools and one privately.[37]

§ Football seems to have been played at this period in other Irish schools besides St Columba's College, including the Royal Schools of Armagh, Dungannon and Portora. A photograph exists of a Trinity team of former Dungannon Royal School boys taken in 1873.[38]

contest in the other.

In the third match in which the Rugby game was played they won an easy victory.

In any case the 1854 foundation date gives Trinity a substantial claim to be the oldest rugby club in continuous existence. Guy's Hospital FC, which was founded in London in 1843 and played its football initially on Kennington Oval, is certainly older, but went into abeyance for some years in the nineteenth century.

Traill was an early stalwart of the Football Club, as were Arthur Palmer, a fellow and distinguished Latinist; the mathematician and Celtic scholar Charles Graves, a fellow until consecrated Bishop of Limerick in 1866; and Graves's three sons, Alfred, Arnold, and Charles. Alfred was a collector of Irish music and the composer of 'Father O'Flynn', while Arnold was an international cricketer, a champion hurdler, and a leading proponent of technical education in Ireland. But the most remarkable of the pioneers, and the one who deserves to be known as the father of Irish rugby, was Charles Burton Barrington, who captained the club for three years from 1867 to 1870.

Barrington's uncle, Charles West*, was a footballer, and it is possible that he influenced the game in the university. 'Charley West', wrote Barrington, 'was at Rugby and is the "East" in *Tom Brown's Schooldays*. He might have had a hand in it, but he would have been before 1850.'[39] Giving his own early reactions to football in Trinity, Barrington remarked: 'When this Rugbean went out to play in the [College] Park for the first time the game may have seemed to him peculiar but it never occurred to him that it was anything else than Rugby of sorts.'[40] He retained this impression although 'the whole thing was very loose, two fellows were made heads. Tossed for first choice and then picked their team from the bystanders who happened to turn up.'[41]

Barrington had been introduced to football at St Columba's College, where

we played a sort of soccer game. On one afternoon a man called Strickland appeared and played in our game. He belonged to the T. C. D. football club, we heard, but who brought him the boys did not know. He played as we did. On making a catch, though, he ran with the ball, but when collared and downed would not let the ball go. Our big boys had difficulty in getting it from him. This incident would show that

---

* Charles Burton West entered Trinity in 1844, graduating in 1849.

T. C. D. did run with the ball in 1859. Anyhow our Masters made him drop it . . . [42]

While on holiday from his English public school in 1863, Barrington had played a match in Merrion Square with several other Rugbeans who were in Dublin, but it was not a success.[43] Having completed his schooling he entered Trinity in January 1867, where, he discovered, things were not as they should have been, for there were 'no cycles, no golf, no hockey, no anything,' only card-playing, billiards, whiskey-drinking, and a stilted social life. There was, however,

a little desultory football, with no particular rules to speak [of], or kit. A good little chap called Wall was running this show. I started away and pulled things together, made a good club out of it with the rules of Rugby School, and we were very successful for it caught on at once. I have a photo of our First XV by me, and we are a queer-looking lot judged by modern ideas. We had caps made in Rugby too, but there was no-one in those far-off times to play against. The match of the year was against the Medical School. Sometimes too the Dublin Garrison boiled up a team to play us . . . We played matches among ourselves, 'pick up' twice or three times a week . . . The Club was really a great success and did introduce the Rugger game into Ireland.[44]

Barrington goes on to describe how he and the secretary, R. M. Wall (whose father, Rev. F. H. Wall, was headmaster of another early rugby nursery, Arlington School, Portarlington), tackled the problems of dress and rules:

The club had *no rules*, written or unwritten. The[y] just played and ran with the ball, no touch line, no goal lines, our only parpanalia [*sic*] being the Rugby goal posts. These were all sufficient for the simple tastes of those days in Dublin Football. A Rugbean brought in the new idea of Rules. Rugby [School] itself though had no written rules! . . . They were *traditional*, like the British Constitution or the Secrets of Free Masonry.[45]

In fact Rugby School had produced written rules in 1846, and a further set had been drawn up by Blackheath FC, one of the earliest of English clubs, founded in 1862. But when Barrington and Wall met to draw up rules in the secretary's rooms in Botany Bay early in 1868, the Rugby School tradition was paramount: 'Wall sat gravely at his little table. A small dark wiry hardy chap with a short black beard and kindly dark eyes. He wrote and I dictated. Gradually and gradually as one could remember them the unwritten laws that govern the immortal Rugby game were put on paper.'[46] It is interesting to observe how the pattern of the modern game was already established by 1868:

D.U. LAWS OF FOOTBALL

(1) The kick-off from the middle must be a place-kick.

(2) Kick-out must be from 25 yards out of goal, not a place-kick.

(3) Charging is fair in case of a place-kick, as soon as the ball has touched the ground; in case of a kick from a catch as soon as the player offers to kick, but he may always draw back, unless he has touched the ball with his foot.

(4) If a player makes a Fair Catch, he shall be entitled to a free kick, provided he claims it, by making a mark with his heel at once; and in order to take such kick he may go back as far as he pleases, and no player on the opposite side shall advance beyond his mark until he has kicked.

(5) A Fair Catch cannot be made from Touch.

(6) A Player is off side when the ball has been kicked, or thrown or knocked on, or is being run with by one of his own side behind him.

(7) A Player off side may impede the game by standing close to the ball; but he may not, in any case, kick or touch it, charge or put over.

(8) A Player is on side when the ball is kicked or thrown or knocked on, or when it has rebounded from the body of any player of the opposite side.

(9) It is not lawful to take up the ball when not in touch, except in an evident hop. Lifting the ball is strictly prohibited.

(10) Running in is allowed to any player on side, provided he does not run through touch.

(11) If in case of a run in, the ball is held in a maul, it shall not be lawful for any other player on his own side to take it from the runner and run with it.

(12) It shall be lawful for any player to call upon any other player, holding the ball in a maul, to put it down, when evidently unable to get away.

(13) A Player, if he wishes to enter a maul, must do so on side.

(14) No Player, out of a maul, may be held or pulled over, unless he himself is holding the ball.

(15) No hacking, as distinct from Tripping, is fair.

(16) Try at Goal. A ball touched between the goal posts may be brought up to either of them, but not between.

(17) When the ball has been touched down behind the goal, the player who touched it down is entitled to walk out straight 25 yards, and any one of his side may take a place-kick, but as soon as the ball has been placed, the opposite side may charge.

(18) It shall be a goal if the ball be dropped, but not if punted, hit or thrown, between the posts or posts produced at any height over horizontal bar, whether it touch it or not.

(19) No goal may be kicked from touch.

(20) A Ball in Touch is dead; consequently, the first player on his side must, in any case, touch it down, bring it to the side of touch, and throw it straight out.

27

(21) Holding and throttling is disallowed.

(22) Sneaking in opponents' goal is discountenanced.

(23) The Captains of sides, or any two deputed by them, shall be the sole arbiters of all disputes.

No law may be altered or made unless at least a week's notice be given of a meeting, and such meeting shall consist of at least 20 members or more.

Drawn Up by C. B. Barrington and R. M. Wall, 16 T. C. D., Jan. 1868.

Rule 15, prohibiting hacking, represented an important difference between the football played in Rugby School and at Trinity College. Barrington described the hacking practised in the school:

In those days no-one was allowed to put his head down in the scrum, if he did it was immediately pulled up again by the others. The forwards all stood straight up hacking away for all they were worth at the opposite side. All standing straight up, packed close together and wearing very heavy boots. The only swing in their kicks being made with their jerking heads. This may seem a bit of an Irish way of putting it. Before my time they had what was called a Hallelujah at the end of a House Match ... *The ball was then taken away.* All the players went into the scrum and hacked each other away dutifully for five minutes. That was the finish and all went to their houses to hot water, footpans, tea and baked potatoes. The latter being a treat in a House Match always.[47]

Writing to Watson in 1930, Barrington remarked that the front of his tibia even then had a 'saw-like edge' from this practice.

Dress, too, was selected by captain and secretary, as Barrington later explained:

Little Wall and myself sat in conclave in his rooms in Botany Bay and on the lines of Rugby custom drew up the schemes. We introduced, however, knickerbockers in lieu of flannels–this was done out of respect for the black earth of our College Park. We decided on the colour being Red and Black for the very same reason.[48]

The committee accepted these proposals without demur, and the arrival of the new kit, which had been ordered from Rugby, caused quite a stir in the college, as formal uniforms for football were a novel idea in Ireland. Highly delighted with his new outfit, Barrington dressed and proceeded to Fitzwilliam Square,

to let my dear mother see her son in this resplendent appurtenance. She was at luncheon and Aunt Josephine was with her–a very pretty lady, daughter of Sir Matthew Barrington. Her back was towards me as she sat at table. I stooped down and kissed her. 'Look at *this*, Aunt Jo.' She turned round and seeing the red and black and huge rough-looking person gave a terrified scream and then began to sob and cry, 'Oh, that I should have lived to be kissed by an acrobat!' ... This was the dress of all playing members, and the fifteen wore 'caps'* as a mark of distinction.[49]

In reply to a query from Watson, Barrington explained that the start of the game was more or less as it is today:

The ball was nicely placed on the ground exactly mid-way between the two goals. The forwards lined up each side a respectable distance from the ball. Then at the word of the captain the best kicker he had ran forward and kicked off towards the opponent's goal. If it went into touch the ball was brought back, replaced and kicked off again. Directly the ball was in the air both sides started on their job.[50]

In reply to another question concerning the method of scoring, Barrington explained that a 'touch down' meant touching down the ball in one's own goal in defence:

There were no points in those days ... A 'goal,' a 'try,' a 'touch down' were the points we went by ... A goal off a try and a goal dropped were the only two kinds of goals we had. There was no such thing as a 'penalty goal.' When a misdemeanour was committed the ball was brought back to the spot of the crime, placed on the ground and a scrum formed round it and on again. A goal off a fair catch was the same as a goal dropped. A goal or a try were the real deciding factors. A 'touch down' was only a deciding factor when there was nothing else, but that was not looked up[on] as a real victory.[51]

Barrington recalled that when he played his first match in Trinity in 1867 there was no distinction between forwards or backs, the players all running after the ball. He introduced a full-back and two half-backs, one on either side of the scrum, as at Rugby School.

Further light was thrown on the early manifestations of rugby in Trinity by Barrington's contemporary Arnold Graves:

Some of the rules I remember, hacking was barred but tripping was allowed. Passing was against the rules—it was called hand ball. We played without a referee. There was offside† of course. The scrummages were interminable and lasted until the man holding the ball expressed his willingness to put it down, and that was only when his side was

---

* The caps were red and black quartered, with a gold shamrock on the front, and similar caps with gold shamrocks were worn by first-team members of other clubs. The shamrock was surrendered during the 1880-81 season to become the emblem of the IRFU, and was replaced with the university coat of arms in red and black. An all-white strip for the First Fifteen, with red and black socks, was introduced in 1893-94.
† An early description of hurley in Co. Antrim records, 'Each team had to keep their own side.' The term seems to have originated as the phrase 'off your side'.[52]

losing ground. I have seen a scrummage travel half way down the ground . . . and as there was no passing one often saw very fine long runs–sometimes even three-quarters of the length of the ground, with wonderful swerves and dodges . . . in every respect the game was more individual and scientific than it is today.[53]

Football was such a novelty that on match days Nassau Street railings were lined with spectators, and the bow windows of the Kildare Street Club, known to rumbustious undergraduates as 'cod bank', or, the 'seat of the scornful', were filled with admirers.

The invention of the pneumatic bladder greatly assisted the handling game, and in November 1872 the club adopted an 'essential change' whereby the ball might be picked up if it were in motion, whether hopping or not; up to this point, as in Gaelic football, the ball could not be picked up off the ground.[54] This furthered the distinction between forwards and backs, who were now divided into quarter-backs, half-backs, threequarter-backs, and a full-back.

The college in Barrington's time was not lacking in its share of characters. One medical contemporary, Molony, was 'a tall thin wiry man, getting a bit grey over the ears. Clean shaved and a big moustache. A lined face and a tanned skin . . . He was taking out his degree to marry some Princess in foreign parts as there was no medical man in her kingdom!'[55]

Barrington and his brother Croker were formidable oarsmen. Another of his colleagues, Bram Stoker–later Henry Irving's secretary and the creator of Dracula–was 'a big strong awkward chap rowing in the four at No. 3. His mother, keeping up along the wall on a car, called out, "They'll be beaten–none of them is keeping stroke with Abraham!" '[56] J.J. Digges La Touche, another contemporary, was a 'hardy, wiry little chap and a strict and unmerciful task-master if over one in a boat. His tongue too was as long as his name! I don't suppose he weighed 7 stone.'[57]

An unfortunate army officer, Dutting, broke his leg during a match between DUFC and the Garrison.

The game was stopped and poor Dutting was carried by a crowd of medical students into the M[edical] S[chool] and gently deposited on the big table in the centre of the demonstration room under the big glass toplight. It was a time of delight for our budding medicos–a real live man on the table for them and no professor to interfere. Sam Haughton turned up with all his dogs, but they would not let him touch the patient. [Eventually] Bennett, the professor of anatomy, was sent for and did the job first rate.* The man quite recovered, but it was always said that he could never forget that match against T. C. D.[58]

No Dublin club was allowed to play the Trinity First Fifteen without first defeating the second team. The first fixture to be played outside Dublin was against the North of Ireland Football Club, Belfast, in 1871. In December 1873 the club made the first of many journeys across the Irish Sea to play the Dingle Club of Liverpool under the 'new' Rugby Union rules; and when Dingle made the return journey, the match in College Park attracted a crowd of three thousand. The urge to play at international level was already developing. A meeting of DUFC was held twelve months later to arrange a game between Ireland and England, at which the secretary read a letter from the secretary of the English Rugby Union (formed in 1871) suggesting dates for the match in the following February. It was agreed that a representative committee be formed and that a date could then be agreed upon.[59] The other clubs were notified, and nominated their representatives. This meeting was held in the Grafton Street premises of the sports supplier John Lawrence, editor of the celebrated *Handbook of Cricket in Ireland*. Dublin University, Wanderers, Lansdowne, Bray, Engineers, Portora Royal School, Dungannon Royal School and Monaghan were represented, many delegates of the other clubs also being Trinity men.[60] Significantly, the most prominent of the Belfast clubs, North of Ireland FC, was not represented at this meeting.

Following the meeting a circular was issued to the clubs and to the press, acknowledging the role that the Rugby Union was playing as the representative organisation in England, and seeking support for the fledgling Irish Football Union. The circular suggested the establishment of interprovincial and North v. South fixtures, and a February date for the forthcoming fixture with England.[61] (The initial game at Kennington Oval was won by England, before three thousand spectators, by two goals and a try to nil.)

Before this game took place, a meeting was held in Belfast in January at which a Northern Football Union was formed. It was agreed to offer 'physical assistance' to Ireland in the forthcoming international, and a Belfast v. Dublin challenge was arranged for

* Haughton, professor of geology, was an expert in animal mechanics. E. H. Bennett, the university anatomist, later became professor of surgery.

later in the season.[62]

The two unions merged to form the Irish Rugby Football Union in 1879. The crucial meeting was held in no. 9, Trinity College, where after much discussion – in which a prominent part was played by W. C. Neville of DUFC (a pioneer obstetrician who captained Ireland in 1879 and was later president of the union), J. G. Cronyn of DUFC, and W. J. Goulding, a Corkman – the three provinces of Ulster, Leinster and Munster agreed to form the IRFU. According to Cronyn's somewhat laconic description of this historic occasion, 'Goulding, Neville and myself did most of the talking and eventually we wore out the North!'[63]

Besides providing a large membership of the committee of the newly-formed union, Trinity provided the captain and eight other members of the Irish team of twenty, attired in green-and-white striped jerseys, white shorts and green-and-white stockings, that took the field against twenty Englishmen at Kennington Oval in 1875. 'Would it surprise you to hear', asked J. G. Cronyn in a letter to Watson (Cronyn's brother A. P. played on the team), 'that the Selection Committee for the first match met in Trinity and before doing anything else elected themselves *en masse*? If there was no room for a back he went on as a forward!'[64]

These first DUFC men to win representative honours were the initiators of a long tradition, for over one hundred and fifty members of the club have played rugby for Ireland (more than in any other Irish club); the club has also produced English, Welsh and South African internationals. Trinity has also supplied many presidents of the IRFU, one of whom, George Scriven, sensibly ensured that, in the season in which he held office (1882-83) he was also an international selector and captain of the Irish team!

THE HURLEY CLUB

The game of hurley, or hurling,* has been played in Ireland for over a thousand years, as evidenced by frequent references to the sport in Irish literature. All stick-and-ball games may have a common origin, and it is tempting to speculate that hurling, shinty, golf, cricket, hockey, ice hockey, bandy,† croquet, baseball

---

* The sport is always referred to as 'hurley' in the Trinity records.

† Bandy developed in East Anglia as a form of hockey played on ice. It is popular in Scandinavia where it is played with a ball rather than the puck of ice-hockey.

and rounders* may all be related. A poem by Samuel Rowland, which includes an amusing enumeration of Elizabethan pastimes, indicates Irish influence on English games:

> Man, I doe challenge thee to throw the sledge,
> To jumpe or leape over ditch or hedge,
> To wrestle, play at stooleball,† or to runne,
> To pitch the cane, or shoot off a gunne;
> To play at loggets,‡ nine holes or ten pinnes,
> To try it out at football by the shinnes,
> At tick-tacke,§ Irish noddie,‖ man and ruffe,¶
> At hot-cockles,** leap frogge, or blindman buffe.[65]

The sporting connection between the two countries has been remarked upon by many other commentators. In 1527 the Corporation of Galway forbade, among other things, the 'horlinge of the litill balle with hockie stickes.'[66] Arthur Young, on his visit to Ireland in 1780, describes an agile display of hurling as 'the cricket of savages';[67] while an Irish poet of fifty years later calls cricket *iomáint ghallda*, or foreign hurling.[68]

There appear to have been two types of hurling played in Ireland up to the nineteenth century, probably with a common origin but recognizably different. The northern version, *camánacht* or 'commons', resembling modern shinty, was played in winter using a stick with a thin boss cut perhaps from a gorse bush,[69] the ball being hit mainly on the ground; while in the southern version, *iomáin*, the boss was thicker, as in the modern game, the ball was played frequently in the air, and matches took place over the summer months.

There are references to hurley being played in Trinity about 1810 and in 1830;[70] as with cricket and football, these would have been informal games. Along with all other rural pastimes, the traditional game of hurley declined markedly after the Famine, but vestiges had survived and would have been familiar to students of the 1860s. Only two years after the drafting of the rules of football, Lawrence's *Handbook of Cricket in Ireland* (1870-

---

* A children's game, handed down from one generation to the next, whose similarity to baseball is too great to be a coincidence.
† A precursor of cricket.
‡ A form of quoits.
§ Tig or tag.
‖ A card game resembling cribbage.
¶ A card game also called trump.
** A variant of blind man's buff.

71) contains rules drawn up by the Dublin University Hurley Club, together with a statement that English clubs had been enquiring from Lawrence about the rules of the game.

D.U. LAWS OF HURLEY

(1) A player is on side, so long as the ball is on the right side of his person, and he hits it with the left side of his hurl. It is not meant, however, by this rule to prevent a player using both sides of his hurl, whilst dodging the ball; although in doing so he renders himself liable to be shinned. Swiping with the right side is strictly forbidden.

(2) No hurl to be shod with iron, or hooped with wire in a dangerous manner.

(3) No hurl to exceed two inches in depth of blade.

(4) The ball may be taken ten yards in *front* of goal, and then hit off by the goal-keeper, who shall have an unmolested swipe at the ball. No opponent shall be allowed to touch the ball, until the hurl of the goal-keeper shall have done so.

(5) No goal can be obtained in one puck, unless the ball strike an opponent's hurl.

(6) Should the ball be kicked in or hit behind, it may be brought out ten yards in *front* of goal, and hit off again. But if the ball be kicked by a player into his own goal, it shall count for the other side. If the ball be designedly played behind, it shall be considered as still in play.

(7) Should the ball go out of bounds, the first player who shall touch it, either with his hurl or person, shall have the privilege of throwing it out at the place where it intersected the boundary line. If the throw be manifestly partial, the ball shall be returned. The player may not take it himself.

(8) Pushing a man when on side is forbidden.

(9) Running the ball into touch, unless when the goal is eminently threatened, is discountenanced as opposed to straightforward play.

(10) Should a player catch the ball in the air off any enemy's hurl, he can take a free high-up at the place where he stands, but the moment the ball falls on the ground this privilege ceases.

(11) Should a goal-keeper, though warned, advance more than 30 yards in front of goal, an opponent may go behind him and still obtain a goal.

(12) A player shall not be allowed to wind his hurl round his head when in close quarters.

(13) Coming behind off-side to crook an enemy's hurl, whilst he is in the act of striking, is discountenanced as dangerous.

(14) All disputes about infringement of Rules, etc., shall be referred to the committee, five of whom shall form a quorum, whose decision shall be final.

(15) Gentlemen must all appear in some coloured garment on match days. Members of the eleven and fifteen must wear their uniforms.

(16) The ball shall always be the object of play.

Rule 3, concerning the dimensions of the stick, and the extant photographs of the university hurley teams, indicate that the stick used was of the narrow-boss variety. The fact that hurley was a winter game in Trinity is a further indication that the university had adopted the northern version *camánacht*. Rule 1, however, outlawing hitting with the right side of the hurl, seems to have been borrowed from hockey rules then being formulated in England.

As with the Football Club, most of the early matches (which consisted of four quarters of twenty minutes each) seem to have been internal ones, such as Leinster versus the Other Provinces, or the Hurley Eleven versus the Rest of the Field; but after a few years the game had spread to a number of Protestant schools, the Royal Bank, and half a dozen or so other clubs. Pupils in the schools concerned – the King's Hospital, the High School, and the Kingstown, Rathmines, and Santry Schools – matriculated to, and staff were drawn from, Trinity College; and among the clubs, Leinster,* Merrion, Phoenix and Kenilworth were linked to existing cricket clubs with which the university had regular fixtures. But even though an Irish Hurley Union was founded at a meeting held at no. 17, Trinity College, in 1879, 'in consequence of the progress which hurley has made in the past ten years,' its jurisdiction never extended outside a small group of clubs closely associated with the university, and all, unlike the early football clubs, situated near Dublin.

At this meeting the secretary was directed to apply to the Blackheath, Surbiton and Rossall School Hurley Clubs for copies of their rules for consideration.[72] The game in England was then called hockey (although in certain contexts the terms seem to have been used interchangeably†), and a Hockey Union had been formed in 1876; but it was not for another ten years, with the formation of the Hockey Association, that the English game came to be codified.

Armed with this extra information, the university club drew

---

* The Leinster Hurley and Baseball Club.[71]

† Edward Carson, the future Unionist leader, who had been educated at Arlington School, is described as a member of the University Hurley Club.[73] Alfred Perceval Graves and John Ross, who studied in Trinity in this era, both later described themselves as members of the Hockey Club. The game they played was hurley.[74]

THE BOLD COLLEGIANS

up a further set of rules, which were published in Lawrence's *Handbook of Cricket in Ireland* (1879) (appendix 5). Features of these rules are the dimensions of the goals (rule 1) and the stipulation (presumably borrowed from England) in rule 5 that a goal could not be scored directly by a player more than fifteen yards from the end line. The Hurley Union drew up a further set of rules in 1882[75] (appendix 6). The substantial amendments to the university rules drawn up three years earlier permitted stopping with the foot, but not kicking, and handling by the full-back but by no other player.

In spite of the formation of the Irish Hurley Union (or perhaps because of it), by 1882 opposition had arisen to a game that, whatever its antecedents, looked to England for guidance. No doubt this was to some extent politically inspired, for at the time the Home Rule movement, which would not have been widely supported in Trinity, was gathering strength. However, advocates of a related game, boasting a more ancient lineage, were unlikely to be attracted to a university club which aimed at 'reducing the swiping game of the savage to a scientific recreation which may be indulged in ... without being in constant dread of having one's brains dashed by an adversary's hurl.'[76]

In 1884, membership having fallen below the requisite minimum of thirty, the Hurley Club's affiliation to the recently-formed Dublin University Athletic Union lapsed.[77] Thus the game of hurley petered out in Trinity precisely as Michael Cusack was founding the Dublin Hurling Club to re-establish the southern form of the game, which he roundly asserted to be the 'national game of hurling'. As it was agreed that this new club should not be antagonistic to any outdoor sport or form of athletics, former Trinity hurlers may have practised and played with Cusack's club. Dublin University Hockey Club today proudly wears the colours of green and black that passed to it with the mantle of the Hurley Club, which did so much to preserve the northern form of hurling in the dark days after the Famine.*

---

* When hurling was revived in the college and the club resuscitated in the 1950s, Trinity pioneered a series of hurling / shinty matches with the Scottish Universities, beginning in 1964.

11

3

The College Races
and the Athletic Union

Running, jumping, wrestling and throwing have been the prerogative of young men since time immemorial; and according to legend, Irish youth placed great store in its athletic prowess. Modern formalized athletic competition, however, originated in English public schools and universities. The first such athletic meeting was organized by the Royal Military Academy, Woolwich, in 1849; Exeter College, Oxford, followed suit in 1850.

The first modern athletic meeting in Ireland was held in College Park in 1857, organized by the Football Club, which had come into existence three years earlier. Sonorously entitled the 'Dublin University Football Club Foot Races', a series of events was held that, besides a number of races, included dropping the football, throwing the cricket ball, and a cigar race, which contestants had to run with a lighted cigar.

This meeting, held on Saturday 28 February, was attended by the Lord Lieutenant and by crowds so much larger than anticipated that a second meeting, along similar lines, was held within a month. The organization of these events, although officially in the hands of the Football Club, was taken over by an Athletic Committee representative of wider interests, and the origins of formal Trinity athletics go back to the first of these two meetings.* The event became an annual affair, known as the College Races, and its organization was no mean task, because the social popularity of the occasion regularly threatened to swamp the athletics.

Records of the proceedings of the organizing committee sur-

* However, the Dublin University Athletic Club was formally constituted in 1885, to affiliate to the Irish Amateur Athletic Association set up to confront Cusack's GAA.

vive from 1866 and give a vivid picture of the difficulty of arranging a major athletic meeting in the College Park,[1] which at that time had no pavilion and no spectator accommodation. Marquees and seating had to be put up to cope with athletes and spectators (sometimes numbering 20,000) who flooded in to view the sports. There were problems with distributing tickets (a membership scheme had to be devised), with handicapping the races, with communicating the results (a telegraph board was erected), and with keeping the spectators away from the track. There was constant bickering about prizes, which were handsome indeed,* but the music of a couple of military bands helped to soothe the nerves of exhausted competitors, harassed judges, and irritated spectators.

'Jumping with a pole' was added to the programme in 1866, and a seven-mile walking race held the following day.[3] Inevitably, in 1867, the races became a two-day affair, but it was resolved 'That the second day be not as grand as the first', only seven events being held on the second day compared with twelve on the first.[4]

Financially the races were, from the very start, a huge success. An income that regularly exceeded £400 led to a handsome profit, and the accumulated surplus was available for the provision of proper sports facilities, such as the Gymnasium in 1869 and the Pavilion fifteen years later. The meetings of the Athletic Committee were regularly chaired by Traill, Mahaffy, Barrington, or Bram Stoker. Within a few years, the 42-lb shot (a traditional Irish weight) had been replaced by the 16-lb model (enquiries having been made of the English universities);[5] the 'long jump with trapeze' was dropped,[6] and a 'Siamese' race added to the programme.[7] It was resolved that 'all sprint races should be started by word of mouth and long races by pistol'.[8] On a more mundane level, the horses rolling the ground were supplied with the proper boots.[9]

Unlike the form of hurling played in Trinity, athletics was quick to spread outside the walls. The Civil Service Athletic

---

* The prizes for 1883 included a silver challenge cup, a dressing-case, a writing-desk, a claret jug, a Gladstone bag, a silver salver, a clock with aneroid barometer, a brass writing-set, a salt-cellar set, a biscuit box, opera glasses, a silver epergne, an Egyptian beer jug, a dessert case, an oak salad bowl, a crocodile ink-stand, and a pickle frame.[2]

Club was founded in Dublin in 1867; and a few years later cricket clubs, which were widespread, were running athletic meetings around the country. The Irish Champion Athletic Club, originally styled the Royal Irish Athletic Club, was founded by a Trinity man, H. W. D. Dunlop, an outstanding 'pedestrian', in 1872, to organize the premier championship in Irish athletics. The first ICAC meeting was held in College Park the following year; and when Queen's College, Cork, proposed the holding of intervarsity sports, Trinity opposed the idea on the ground that it would interfere with the arrangements of ICAC.[10] Thus the first Irish intervarsity athletic meeting, in 1873, took place without Trinity's participation.

One of the drawbacks of athletics in College Park was the lack of a proper 'running path', and a number of proposals were made for construction of a cinder track.[11] But this would have conflicted with the use made by other clubs of the grass area; and the matter was effectively settled by a resolution passed at the annual meeting of the Football Club in 1872: 'That in the opinion of the meeting the construction of a running path along the side of the football field would be highly detrimental to the interests of the club.'[12] The matter was clearly a contentious one, because a motion put to the annual meeting of the Athletic Club (which succeeded the Foot Races Committee) to construct a running path was eventually defeated only by 27 votes to 26.[13]*

The 1870s and 1880s saw an unprecedented expansion in organized games and in the number of spectators who came to

* Dunlop had been an advocate of the running path proposal and had effected a number of significant improvements (including the reversal of the orientation of the grass track) in the layout of College Park.[14] The Board subsequently refused ICAC permission to use the park. Although the club's officers were mainly Trinity men, it had no formal connection with the college, and Dunlop was forced to look elsewhere. Regarding itself as 'a National Club and not the product of mere rivalry',[15] ICAC aimed to lease some land 'of which the centre will be a cricket ground and the remainder used for the laying down of a proper "cinder running path" now recognized as essential for really good athletic performances'.[16] Having investigated premises at Sydney Parade and Sandymount, Dunlop obtained a 69-year lease from the Earl of Pembroke of ground 'near Lansdowne Road Station', and proceeded to develop a sporting complex with facilities for tennis, archery, cricket, croquet, and football, as well as a cinder track. Thus the Lansdowne Football Club (1872), initially composed principally of Trinity men, has athletic origins. ICAC was dissolved in 1881, its last days marred by a financial dispute involving Michael Cusack.[17] Since 1907 the Lansdowne Road ground has been the headquarters of the Irish Rugby Football Union.

watch them. But the College Races had a social cachet, and in 1873 the editor of the *Irish Sportsman*, a Trinity graduate, W. J. Dunbar, unblushingly pronounced them 'the most important and fashionable gathering for athletic purposes in the world'.[18] A trainer was employed from the London Athletic Club at 15 shillings a day.[19] One of the most coveted prizes was that awarded to the 'Queen of Beauty'.[20]

Some idea of the pressure on attendance, and of the social standing of the guests, may be gleaned from the committee's list of complimentary invitations, which were issued in that year to 'the Provost, Chancellor, Fellows, Professors, the Lord Mayor, Colonels of Regiments, Officers of Regiments and Men of War, the Law Officers, University Members of Parliament, Resident Peers and County "Swells," Officers of Athletic Clubs, Editors of Newspapers, Judges and Handicappers'.[21] On a cautionary note it was added that 'college porters, skips *et hoc genus omne* were to receive as few free tickets as possible.'

The *Illustrated London News* of one year later suggests that 37,000 tickets were sold over the two days,[22] and while this may have been an exaggeration, the problems of coping with such multitudes in College Park were never effectively overcome. Matters nearly came to a head in 1877. The editor of the *Irish Sportsman* went on the attack, describing the official stewards as 'very unworthy successors of the men who made Trinity Athletics something of which the nation might be proud'. The article continued with a litany of complaint: the meeting had been advertised in the English press (to entice leading sportsmen from across the water to compete in open events), and the races had degenerated into a 'vulgar means of making money'; the handicapping was unfair;* the distribution of prizes was accompanied by a 'scandalous melée'; worst of all, virtuous lady guests had been brought into forced proximity with the 'nymphs of the pavement'. The sooner the story of the College Races of 1877 was blotted from the record, the report concluded, the better for all concerned.[23]

Trouble had been brewing for a number of years, and had not gone unnoticed by the Board. In March 1877 one crusty senior fellow had tried to have the races abandoned for that particular

* The editor's son, a well-known handicapper, was not officiating at the races.

year.[24] The Board temporized, but informed the Athletic Committee that if 'irregularities such as had occurred in late years' should arise again, they would be forced to order a suspension.[25]

The bad publicity that the subsequent meeting attracted was an ominous portent. The final straw was a riot, involving three or four hundred students, that took place in Botany Bay (a residential square in the college) in 1878 on the second night of the races. Three porters were injured in attempting to restore order, and a carpenter's shop on the west side of the square was gutted by fire.[26] The Board reacted swiftly and sternly. Miscreants were sent down, prevented from graduating, suspended, fined, or simply admonished, depending on the gravity of their offence; and it was made clear that permission would not be granted for the holding of the races in 1879. Finally the Board refused the Athletic Committee permission to hold its annual meeting in the Examination Hall, but later relented, granting the use of a room in the Museum Building.[27]

The Board then tightened its control over the committee by refusing membership to men whose names were not on the college books.[28] Another irritant emerged in March 1880, when the committee's application to hold the races in June was deferred on timetable grounds, the medical professors giving their opinion that 'the holding of the College athletic sports in June combined with the necessity of six weeks' training on the part of the competitors has seriously injured the studies of large numbers of medical students . . . '[29] The Easter vacation was offered as an alternative, but the proposal was turned down as the condition of College Park would not then be suitable.[30]

Further trouble occurred in April, when the Lord Lieutenant, the Duke of Marlborough, was formally leaving Ireland.* As his procession passed in front of the college, a group of high-spirited students perched on the statues outside the front gate released a stream of balloons half filled with flour which showered the police and the bandsmen. The students also lobbed fireworks under the horses' feet, causing them to rear and prance, and one enthusiast (perhaps an aspiring cricketer) managed to throw a squib into the carriage containing the Lord Lieutenant and the

* During the Duke of Marlborough's period as Lord Lieutenant of Ireland (1876-80) his son, Randolph Churchill, acted as his private secretary. Thus the duke's grandson, Winston, born in 1874, spent his formative years in the Phoenix Park.

Duchess of Marlborough.[31] In the light of this fresh disturbance permission was withheld for the holding of the races in 1880,[32] and the Athletic Committee promptly petitioned the Board that the college gates be closed on the arrival of the duke's successor, 'to prevent the intrusion of the Dublin mob and the consequent disturbances which would be visited on the Athletic Club'.[33]

By this time, in spite of strenuous efforts behind the scenes by Edward Gibson (the Irish Attorney-General) and David Plunket (one of the college's representatives in Parliament, and a founder-member of the Football Club), all hopes for a resumption of the races in that particular year were gone. At a stormy annual meeting of the club held on 26 May the use of Lansdowne Road as a possible venue was mooted, and an ill-judged and ill-tempered letter was composed, asking the Board 'whether it was their intention in future to prevent the College Races being held in the College Park and whether, in future, the members of the Dublin University Athletic Club are in their opinion to be responsible for the conduct of the College students'.[34]

In their reply, the Board expressed their 'disapprobation of the tone of that letter', suggesting that the proceedings of the meeting (held in the Examination Hall and reported in the press) had been 'disrespectful to the authorities of the College and injurious to discipline'. They went on to emphasize the pious (and apparently unfulfilled) hope that the granting of College Park for sporting purposes would have led to an improvement in student behaviour. Finally, however, the Board signalled their intention of allowing the races to continue in 1881, subject to a number of conditions: that there be only a one-day meeting; that committee members be on the college books; that tickets, up to a maximum of 10,000, be sold to members only (members to be responsible for the behaviour of their guests); and that the whole affair be under the supervision of the Junior Dean. The club gratefully seized the olive branch, apologizing for the remarks made 'in the heat of the moment' to which the Board had taken exception.[35]

In the midst of all this *sturm und drang*, sport in the college was making substantial headway. In 1870 the Boat Club became the first Irish club to compete in the Henley Regatta. A four including the Barrington brothers won the Visitors' Cup in 1870 and 1873, and further Boat Club victories came in the Ladies' Plate in 1875 and the Wyfold in 1881; in 1903 the Thames Cup went to a Boat Club eight. The Rowing Club became the first Trinity club to compete in America when a crew was dispatched to take part in the Philadelphia Centennial Regatta in 1876. The four, with the Barrington brothers (who, on graduation, had transferred their allegiance), found the centennial temperatures too much of a handicap, but were successful in a competition restricted to graduates in which they emerged as the only eligible crew!

Some of the great deeds of the pristine Trinity cricketers have already been recorded. The most important development, at the turn of the century, was the Football Club's removal to the north side of College Park. This led not only to a marked improvement in the outfield but to the proper development of the 'square', as more ground was then available for the preparation of wickets. The present square, which is large by any standards, stretches sixty-five yards across the park. During Trinity Term, except for the examination period, cricket is played almost daily, unless athletic contests are scheduled. A vigorous ladies' club was reactivated in 1972;* and it is rare for College Park on a fine evening in May or June to be without an athletic meeting or a cricket match.

These improvements and the college's city-centre site ensured that College Park became the venue for most representative cricket. One of the strongest elevens ever to visit Ireland was the 1905 Australian team, which included Victor Trumper, Kelly, Armstrong, and Cotter. For a University Past and Present Eleven, F. H. Browning scored two half-centuries, T. A. Harvey (who had caught and bowled Grace first ball for a duck on the Great Man's last appearance in Trinity) took six wickets in the match, and Philip Meldon ten; but the Australians won easily. G. J. Meldon was a prolific scorer who took a century off Grace's London County team of 1903, while R. A. Lloyd and H. M. Read (better known for their exploits in another code) contributed twelve centuries to the Trinity score books. Read and Lloyd, who regularly opened the innings, set the record for the club's highest stand when they put on 323 for the first wicket against Co. Kilkenny in 1911.

Besides the numerous international caps won by Trinity

* The Dublin University Women's Cricket Club was founded in 1946,[36] and survived for ten years, going into abeyance through lack of opposition.

footballers, the club has provided eleven players who captained the Irish rugby team while still playing for the university: G. H. Stack, who captained the first Irish side at the Oval in 1874; R. Galbraith (1877); W. C. Neville (1879); G. Scriven (1883); J. G. Franks (1899); H. H. Corley (1902-03); J. C. Parke (1906-08); H. Thrift (1908); R. A. Lloyd (1912-14 and 1920); J. P. Quinn (1914); and J. K. S. Thompson (1923). M. Johnston (1886) and M. Sugden (1931) captained Ireland after their Trinity days were over.

The Leinster Cup competition was first competed for in 1881-82. Trinity won, but as two of the competing clubs had not paid their subscriptions, no cup was available for presentation. This was rectified in the following season, and the cup was presented to Trinity, who conveniently ended up as winners for the second time. Having won the trophy on twenty-two occasions, Trinity shares with Lansdowne FC the honour of having most successes in the competition.

University matches naturally occupy a prominent place in the fixture list of DUFC. Cambridge was the first university side to visit Trinity, in 1878, but the game was cancelled on account of frost. Thus it was not until 1882 that intercollegiate contests took place, with matches against Queen's College, Belfast, Edinburgh University, and Queen's College, Cork. Trinity has long-standing fixtures with both Oxford and Cambridge, in which the honours have been fairly evenly divided. The Dudley Cup for intervarsity competition in Ireland was presented by the Lord Lieutenant, Lord Dudley, in 1904 (but, rumour has it, was never paid for!). The revival of the competition for this famous trophy in 1976 has cemented DUFC's already close relationships with other Irish university clubs.

The first Trinity fixture with a team from outside Britain and Ireland took place in 1888, when the university drew with the New Zealand Maoris (two of whom played barefoot), who had already defeated an Irish fifteen. Another famous match took place in College Park in 1899. The visitors were the Stade Français, the first French team to visit Ireland, and Trinity won the match by a goal and a dropped goal to nil. The French had not at the time mastered the art of drop-kicking, and when R. M. Gwynn dropped a goal he was astonished to receive a kiss from the admiring French captain!

The Football Club has since its inception produced, and

happily still produces, many players of international calibre. F. H. Browning and A. P. Gwynn, fine cricketers, were also half-backs of the highest class. D. B. Walkington was one of the best Irish full-backs of his day. Activities on the field did not prevent him wearing a monocle, which he let fall from his eye as he made the tackle. L. H. Gwynn was another cricketer who was a brilliant threequarter; while J. C. Parke and H. Thrift formed a centre-wing combination for Trinity, and Ireland, that has rarely been equalled. Both excelled at other sports, Parke being Ireland's finest tennis player, while Thrift was a sprinter of international class. Both men captained the Irish Fifteen, in which Parke's strength and timing were complemented by Thrift's fleetness of foot.

Of the many distinguished Trinity half-back pairings, H. M. Read and R. A. Lloyd, who played for Trinity and Ireland just before the First World War, must take the crown. Read and Lloyd were the first pair to distinguish between the roles of scrum-half and out-half: until their arrival, the first half-back up to the scrummage put in and passed the ball. Read was a scrum-half with a swift break and an accurate pass, while Lloyd on his outside was perhaps the finest kicker that Irish rugby has produced, a master of dropped goal, place-kick, and punt, and an outstanding tactician. In 1911 Read captained Trinity in rugby, cricket, and tennis, besides playing for Ireland in all three sports; he became president of the IRFU in 1955-56. Lloyd, who captained Ireland for three seasons before the war, was recalled to the international side as captain in 1920. The back line of the 1912-13 Trinity team, with Read and Lloyd at half-back, consisted entirely of Irish internationals.

C. V. Rooke, captain of DUFC in 1893-94, is one of those credited with developing the role of the modern flank forward. On one occasion, in an international match in Wales, the red-headed Rooke's predatory instincts caused such havoc amongst the Welsh backs that outraged supporters, unused to such tactics, were roused to shout, 'Get back into the scrum, Ginger! You're no forward!' Another outstanding forward, and a famous medical man, Bethel Solomons, captained the university in 1907-08. The First Fifteen won the Leinster Cup and the Second and Third Fifteens (both undefeated) their respective competitions. There was no gainsaying that Trinity was the strongest Irish club, but a good deal of debate arose between the junior teams as to which was the better side. A game was therefore arranged at the end of the season to settle the matter, but the captain, who had not been consulted, announced that his teams would remain undefeated and cancelled the match. Solomons' presence on a successful international side led to a celebrated remark by an inebriated journalist. 'Irish team!' he snorted. 'Call that an Irish team, with fourteen Protestants and one bloody Jew!'

In spite of the decline after 1880 in the status of the College Races, Trinity athletics progressed from strength to strength. The first of a long line of famous runners was A. C. Courtney, who at the College Races of 1873 covered 1000 yards in 2 minutes 23.4 seconds, setting the first world record for a flat race made by an Irishman.[*] In the next decade D. D. Bulger won the Irish 100 yards title six times and the 220 yards, the 120 yards hurdles and the long jump four times each, as well as the British AAA long jump and 120 yards hurdles championships. Bulger was a heavy man, and his fellow-competitors regularly heard a thud, thud, thud as he got up speed and inevitably overhauled them. The two outstanding runners of the early years of the twentieth century were Harry Thrift and G. N. Morphy. Thrift, the Irish 440 champion of 1906, won the 100 yards for seven successive years at the College Races. Morphy was Irish champion in the 440 yards, half-mile and mile on three occasions each.

A Harriers Club for cross-country running was founded in 1886,[†] and a long series of contests against Edinburgh University was instituted in 1903. A Bicycle Club was founded in 1878, when cycling had become a familiar pastime, and Trinity men played a prominent part in the formation of the Irish Cycling Association, the first governing body of Irish cycle racing.[‡]

R. J. Mecredy, who graduated in 1884, was a cyclist in a class

---

[*] This was, in fact, the first recognized world record for a race. The second was also made in Dublin, by Walter Slade, who became the first man to run a half-mile in under two minutes, for England v. Ireland at Lansdowne Road in 1876. Slade later became treasurer of the Rugby Football Union.

[†] The harriers combined with the athletes to form the Dublin University Harriers and Athletic Club in 1921.

[‡] Bicycles were allowed in College Park but forbidden in the Courts.[37] The Bicycle Club was occasionally permitted to play polo on the 'new' rugger pitch,[38] having previously been refused permission to play on the 'old' rugger pitch when not in use by the Cricket Club.[39]

of his own in Trinity and Ireland; his most remarkable feats were never equalled. He was one of the very first schoolboys to ride to school on a bicycle, and in 1879, as a pupil at Portora Royal School in Enniskillen, set out to cycle to Dublin before he had learned how to dismount! Mecredy dominated Irish cycling in the 1880s, but his career was jeopardized by a severe crash, which almost necessitated amputation of a leg, in a race between Trinity and Cambridge in 1885. He returned to action to win the 25-mile English tricycle championship in 1886 and the 5-mile championship in the following year. He became one of the first to appreciate the advantages of Dunlop's pneumatic tyre, first manufactured in Dublin in 1888, and rode on a tricycle to Coventry (the headquarters of the cycle industry) soon after the new tyres had been invented. The pneumatic tyres evoked huge interest, and a crowd of several hundred gathered around his machine within moments of his arrival.[40] Returning to the track, Mecredy won all four English championships on pneumatic tyres in 1890, and went on to win seven more Irish titles as well as the second hundred-mile road race to be held in Ireland. The university club was not confined to undergraduates, and Mecredy won all his championships representing Trinity. When he retired he was able to present his wife with two belts, one consisting entirely of English championship medals and the other of Irish ones. Mecredy later became editor of the *Irish Cyclist*, and wrote several books on cycling and motoring.

The popularity of cycling as a sport declined with the advent of the motor-car after the turn of the century, and the club faded from the records shortly after the First World War, not to be revived until 1987. The last of the great Trinity cyclists was the distinguished Dublin doctor, writer and wit, Oliver St John Gogarty, who, although he never won an Irish title, has left a gripping account of his contests for posterity.[41] Gogarty played soccer with Bohemians FC and was a powerful swimmer who, as a member of the Swimming Club (formed in 1897), was awarded the medal of the Royal Humane Society for saving a life at peril of his own. As a 45-year-old Free State senator he was kidnapped by republicans during the Civil War; he escaped by swimming the Liffey, and later presented the river, in thanksgiving, with a pair of swans.[42]

The Hockey Club, founded with the Irish Hockey Union

in 1893 and proudly sporting the green and black of the old Hurley Club, soon started to produce an outstanding crop of Irish players such as R. F. M. Clifford (centre-half), the 'Trinity catapult', H. E. Rutherfoord (a prolific inside-forward) and A. M. Porter. The latter, a classical scholar and an international cricketer who had captained his university at cricket and his country at hockey, was killed on active service as a volunteer in the Boer War. The Board of Trinity College does not, as a rule, pass resolutions of sympathy, but it was moved to an expression of feeling when the news reached Dublin. Porter is commemorated by the Marshall Porter prize in classics and by a stained-glass window in the Graduates' Memorial Building depicting Epaminondas, the Theban warrior who fell at Mantinea, and Demosthenes, the great Athenian orator.

The Lawn Tennis Club was founded in 1877,* when permission was given to mark out courts in the New Square,† provided that 'the committee of the club make themselves responsible for the orderly conduct of all persons using the grounds for this purpose'.[43] Two years later, with a college subvention of £100 and an input from the club of £150, asphalt courts were laid down in the vicinity of the Gymnasium.[44] In that year the Tennis Club was sufficiently well established to enter a tug-of-war team in the Civil Service Sports!

In the 1890s the standard of tennis in Ireland was on a par with that in England: individual Irish players won championships at Wimbledon, and Irish teams beat their English counterparts on a number of occasions. J. C. Parke, holder of twenty Irish caps as a centre-threequarter, was undoubtedly Ireland's finest tennis player. As an undergraduate he concentrated on rugby, and it was not until he left college that his prowess at tennis became apparent. He won fifteen Irish, three English, two European and one Australian championship, and the mixed doubles title at Wimbledon in 1914. From 1908 to 1914 he represented the British Isles in the Davis Cup and was primarily responsible for winning the cup in Australia in 1912. In the following year he faced the American, M. E. McLoughlin, in the Davis Cup at Wimbledon. McLoughlin's cannonball service struck terror into the hearts of his opponents, forcing them to take the serve standing well

---

* Also the foundation year of the All England and Fitzwilliam Clubs.
† Now the headquarters of the Croquet Club.

behind the base line. McLoughlin had defeated Parke in the men's singles at Wimbledon earlier in the season, and in the second match Parke decided on a change of tactics. Standing well into the court, he took the service on the half-volley, a feat possible only for someone with perfect timing and a wrist of iron. The strategy worked, and his return of service was so swift that Parke gained the upper hand, winning the match by three sets to two.

The first interclub golf match in Ireland, according to the *Irish Sportsman*,[45] took place between the Belfast Club (now Royal Belfast) and the King James VI Golf Club from Perth on the newly-laid golf course in Holywood, Co. Down, in May 1884. The Scots were obviously more skilful and more practised, winning by the modest margin of 57 holes to 8! Dublin University Golf Club, founded ten years later, initially included both staff and students; the indefatigable Dr Traill, who played the game almost at the double, took up golf at the age of fifty-two, smartly reducing his handicap to single figures.

Trinity's most distinguished golfer was Lionel Munn, who won his rugby colours in 1909-10. The Golf Club won the Irish Senior Cup when it was first competed for, in 1900, and again, with Munn in the team, in both 1910 and 1911, defeating Royal Portrush in the latter year on its own famous course by seven matches to nil. Munn won the Irish Amateur Open Championship three times,* the Irish Close Championship on four occasions, and the Belgian Amateur Championship in 1931 and 1932. He retained his skill for many years. In 1937 he was runner-up in the British Amateur Championship, and in 1938, thirty years after he had entered Trinity, was selected to represent Britain and Ireland against America in the Walker Cup. The club was greatly assisted in its early years by the granting of special membership of Royal Dublin to a limited number of students, a tradition that is now happily maintained at the famous Portmarnock club.

The College Races, which in 1857 had been the creation of the Football Club, soon generated a momentum of their own, and came to be organized by an Athletic Committee with representatives of other interests besides football. In 1869 it was decided to devote £60 of the accrued surplus to equipment for the proposed Gymnasium.[46] The Athletic Committee evolved into an

---

* Munn held the record for the longest eighteen-hole match in the Irish Amateur Championship, being defeated in 1908 by C. A. Palmer at the tenth tie hole.

Athletic Club, and in 1881 it was resolved to ask the Board for a committee room and also for the use of the 'indescribable tenement' at the rear of the Museum Building for storage of equipment.[47] At the annual meeting it was reported that the races (which had been suspended in 1879 and 1880) had gone off without a hitch,* and a suggestion was made that the surplus in the club's account be put towards the construction of a pavilion. It was further proposed that an Athletic Union be established, with representatives from all college clubs on its committee, to organize the races, and to make grants to clubs if the surplus in hand exceeded £100.[48]

A set of rules for the Athletic Union was then accepted by a general meeting in February 1882.[49] These may be paraphrased as follows:

1. The colours were to be gold shamrocks on a black background.
2. The Athletic Union was to consist of the following clubs: Boat, Rowing, Cricket, Football, Gymnastic and Lawn Tennis (the two had been combined), Bicycle, Racket, and Hurley. Club membership was restricted to graduates and undergraduates.
3. The committee of the union was made up of a president and vice-president (to be chosen from senior members of the college, including the parliamentary representatives of the university), a secretary, treasurer and two further members, to be elected at the annual general meeting in Hilary Term, and twelve members to be nominated by member-clubs: two each from Boat, Rowing, Cricket and Football, and one each from Bicycle, Gymnastic and Lawn Tennis, Racket, and Hurley.
4. The annual subscription for both graduate and undergraduate members was five shillings, payment entitling a member to buy tickets for the races.
5. The committee was empowered to make grants to the member-clubs from the surplus that had accrued from the College Races, provided that this surplus was maintained at at least £100. The ceiling for 1883 was fixed at £150, and in most years this was the total annual grant to clubs.
6. An amendment, not in the original rules, was added to ensure that clubs with a membership of less than thirty be suspended from the union.[50] (The Hurley Club's membership fell below this level soon after the formation of the union, and in December 1884 it was replaced by the Association Football Club.)

Although the main concern of the new union was the man-

* At an Athletic Club committee meeting of 4 June 1881 it was resolved that 'a Reporter's ticket be not sent' to 'the *Irish Sportsman*'s paper' in consequence of its attitude towards the club in former years.

agement of the College Races, its constitution shows clearly that, as a body representative of the athletic clubs, it was a forerunner of DUCAC. The prudent decision to restrict total annual expenditure on the clubs to a level of £150 meant that funds were accruing that could be used for capital development. At the annual meeting in 1881 it was proposed that the surplus funds be employed to erect the much-needed pavilion,[51] but before this could be done the union needed to get control of the funds currently in the hands of the trustees of the old Athletic Club, amounting to £382; and here the union ran up against the redoubtable Dr Traill.

The rules of the union did not specify the Athletic Club as a member, indicating that this club had been recognized as a representative body for running the College Races rather than as a sports club *per se*. Possibly it was felt that the Athletic Club should develop as a club in its own right; probably Traill intended to use the issue of control of the funds to influence the development of the Athletic Union; in any case an unseemly row ensued in which the advice of senior counsel was sought.[52] The affair was finally resolved in 1884 with the Board's consent to the construction of a Pavilion at the eastern end of the cricket ground.[53]

On 1 March of that year a deputation from the Athletic Union consisting of Fitzgerald, J. H. Jellett FTCD (another sportsman destined to become Provost), and the Honorary Secretary waited on the Board seeking permission to build a Pavilion. The Board, taking a strong line, approved, in principle, the proposal for 'a permanent Pavilion to be erected and maintained in the College Park at the expense, and for the use of, the University Athletic Union', and information was sought concerning estimates, funds in hand, and possible means of obtaining the necessary balance.[54]

Confirmation of this decision was forthcoming in July, when the Board authorized the committee of the Athletic Union to construct a pavilion according to the plans of the architect (Sir Thomas Drew), provided 'that the Bursar is satisfied that the committee have in hands sufficient funds to complete the building externally so that it shall be ornamental as seen from the Park'. The Bursar was to ensure that a contract was drawn up with a 'respectable builder', but (in a telling phrase) was 'not to be responsible to the builder for the erection of the building', so that the cost of £1050 fell entirely upon the Athletic Union, which had £650 on hand. Two of the crustier senior fellows, Carson and Galbraith, dissented on the grounds that the *cista communis* might ultimately be drawn upon, and that an 'interest' was being introduced into the college which 'might well be independent of, and may be opposed to, the Governing Body'.[55]

The onus was now on the Athletic Union to raise the balance of the money required for the building. Some of the money was raised by offering life membership of the union, with perpetual right of admission to the Pavilion; and the architect's plans were modified to match the sum available. In the event Carson and Galbraith's worst fears were justified when, in March of the following year, the Board made a grant of £100 to the building fund, provided that the Bursar was satisfied that the balance had been collected by the Athletic Union.[56] Then in 1893 Samuel Haughton – a fellow famous for his *Principles of Animal Mechanics* and for his calculation of the length of the drop in order to assist the hangman – drew the Board's attention to an even more serious problem, and it was resolved that the 'attention of the Senior and Junior Deans be directed to the abuses which are alleged to exist as regards the consumption of drink in the house known as "the Pavilion" '.* The two officers were urged to take all necessary steps 'to abate the evils complained of at the earliest period'.[57]

---

* A tradition developed that, after the Colours Dance, which followed the Colours Match (the home rugby game versus Oxford or Cambridge), the two teams would proceed to the Pavilion to drink beer and roast sausages until dawn, when, still attired in evening dress, the hosts would accompany their visitors to the Mail Boat.

4

The Gaelic Athletic Association

The last quarter of the nineteenth century was marked by a resurgence of national sentiment in Ireland. The rise of the Land League, and of the Home Rule party under Parnell, presaged a slow but steady change in Anglo-Irish relations, indicating that in Ireland the age of deference was coming to an end. The literary renaissance spearheaded by Yeats and Lady Gregory, and the Gaelic League led by Douglas Hyde, signalled a revival in Irish cultural affairs, a development paralleled in rural life by the emergence of the co-operative movement under Horace Plunkett, preaching a gospel of regeneration and self-help. The rise of self-assertion in Irish sporting life crystallized around the formation of the Gaelic Athletic Association in 1884.

Michael Cusack, the *fons et origo* of the GAA, was an extraordinary figure. An Irish-speaker from the Burren in Co. Clare, he came to Dublin and taught in the French College, Blackrock (forerunner of Blackrock College), moving in 1877 to the centre of Dublin, where he opened the Civil Service Academy at Gardiner Place. The academy took the products of the new system of national education and prepared them intensively (and successfully) for entrance to the civil service, the army and the university. As a youth, and as a teacher, Cusack seems to have taken part in the sports that were common in schools or in the countryside at the time—hurling, football, cricket, athletics and handball—as well as encouraging his pupils to do likewise. He was also active as a member and a judge in the Irish Champion Athletic Club, founded in 1871.

Cusack was a determined nationalist and a member of the Society for the Preservation of the Irish Language, founded in 1876; he was also a visionary, a man of boundless, restless energy, and an experienced athlete, filled with a burning desire to tilt at establishment windmills. His portrait is well known: a burly bearded man complete with knee breeches, a large hat, a dog and a blackthorn stick. He has been immortalized by James Joyce as the 'Citizen' in *Ulysses*: 'seated on a large boulder at the foot of a round tower ... a broadshouldered deepchested stronglimbed frankeyed redhaired freely freckled shaggybearded widemouthed largenosed longheaded deepvoiced barekneed brawnyhanded hairylegged ruddyfaced sinewyarmed hero.'[1] Joyce detested the Irish-language movement, but an impression is left of an easily roused, often violent personality, and of an unrepentant, splenetic propagandist.

Cusack disliked the political trends that he detected in Irish athletics, dominated first by Trinity College and then by the Protestant establishment. In his view an anglicized form of athletics was spreading throughout the country, often through the medium of the cricket clubs. Too much emphasis was placed on 'track' events, such as racing and cycling, which he deemed to be English imports, to the detriment of the traditional Irish field sports such as throwing and jumping. To make matters worse, the organizers of Irish athletics were taking their cue from across the water. (The Amateur Athletic Association had been founded in England in 1880.)

There were two other problems. Sabbatarianism, a striking feature of evangelical Irish Protestantism, dictated that sports meetings in which Protestants took the lead would not be held on Sunday, the traditional day of recreation for rural and Catholic Ireland. Further, the vexed question of the definition of an amateur was debarring the artisan and the labourer from taking their rightful place in organized sport. The following definition of an 'Amateur Sportsman', coined when betting was still rife in most sports,* was given in Lawrence's *Handbook of Cricket in Ireland* (1867-68).

Any person who has never competed in an open competition, or for public money, or for admission money, or with professionals for a prize, public money or admission money, and who has never at any period of his life taught or persisted in the pursuit of athletic exercises as a means of livelihood.[2]

* England's principal athletic stadium at Lillie Bridge in London was wrecked by dissatisfied spectators in 1887 after the cancellation of a race between two leading professional walkers, neither the athletes nor their managers being able to agree on who should win!

The Hurling Club, 1879, with G.F. Fitzgerald, third from right in the back row.

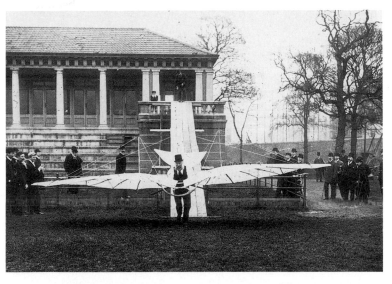

G.F. Fitzgerald in 1895 attempting to fly from a ramp up against the Pavilion in College Park. (Courtesy TCD Physics Department)

The Boat Club IV of 1873.   *A cartoon of J.P. Mahaffy, cricketer.*

A sketch of the College races from the Illustrated London News, *20 June 1874.*
The orientation of the track was the reverse of that at present.

The Irish game of handball, from the Illustrated Sporting and Dramatic News, *16 February 1884.*

A portrait of the Dublin Metropolitan Hurling Club, founded by Michael Cusack, from the Illustrated Sporting and Dramatic News, *22 March 1884.*

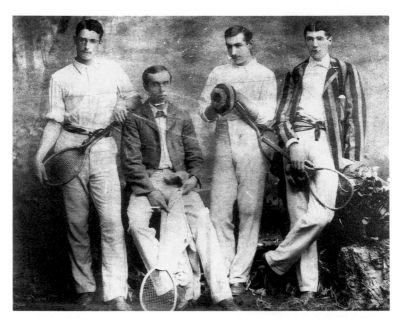

The Lawn Tennis Team, 1886.

The Cycling Club of 1899 with Oliver St John Gogarty standing in the back row on the left. (Courtesy Oliver Gogarty)

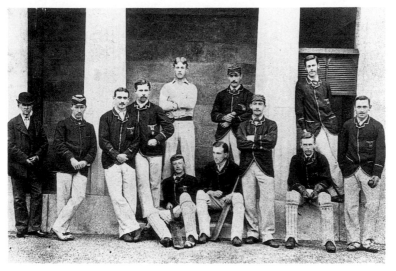

The Cricket Club, 1881.

The Cricket Club v. W.G. Grace's London County XI in the College Park, 1903.

The River Liffey at Islandbridge after the turn of the century, with the Trinity Boathouse and a stand since removed. (Courtesy DU Boat Club)

The Hockey XI captained by D.L.C. Dunlop, winners of the Irish Senior Cup in 1905-06. H.W.D. Dunlop, the captain's father and founder of the Irish Champion Athletic Club, is wearing the top hat.

Samuel Beckett (second from right) and W.S. Cunningham (extreme right) in a foursome at Carrickmines Club in 1927. Beckett played to a seven handicap and retained his connection with the club for many years. (Courtesy W.S. Cunningham)

The combined Trinity and Edinburgh University Ladies' Tennis teams, 1937. (Courtesy W.M. Matthews)

Maeve Kyle setting a UK all-comers' indoor record of 58.3 seconds for the 440 yards in London in 1962. (Courtesy Maeve Kyle)

International lacrosse, Ireland v. Wales, on the rugby pitch in College Park in 1956. Clarissa Crawford is the Irish player on the attack. (Courtesy Clarissa Pilkington)

This definition–which, apart from the final clause, would almost be acceptable today–had undergone crucial changes with the appearance of the 1875-76 edition of the *Handbook*. The term 'Amateur' now read 'Gentleman Amateur', and the ominous phrase 'nor is a mechanic, artisan, or labourer' had been tacked on to the end of the paragraph.[3*] Taken together with the prohibition of Sunday sport, this sadly misguided snobbery ensured that the majority of the population could not participate in amateur sports. Such an attitude, which had already caused dissension in rowing circles, increased the likelihood of a split in Irish athletics.

Following the success of a National Athletic Sports organized in Co. Mayo in 1874 by Pat Nally, a leading athlete and nationalist, Cusack arranged a similar event open to Dublin artisans the following year. In May he organized his own academy's sports meeting in the Phoenix Park, and in July proceeded to win the Irish weight-throwing championship. In a series of articles that appeared in the press in 1881 he made some moderate criticisms of the administration of athletics and rugby in Ireland, suggesting that the organizers make room for a 'strip of green across their colours', and calling for a return to traditional Irish events and the involvement of Irish people in the government of their games.[4] The *Irish Sportsman* was, at the time, arguing strongly for home rule in sporting affairs; Cusack would soon be calling for *sinn féin*!

In 1882-83 he attempted to revive what he believed to be the traditional (southern) form of Irish hurling by founding the Dublin, Academy and Metropolitan Hurling Clubs. Hurling, as Cusack defined it, was played with the broad-bossed stick as distinct from the northern version of the game, more akin to modern shinty, played in Trinity. The initial impetus in Trinity, moreover, had begun to falter: the Hurley Club, its membership having fallen below the level of thirty stipulated in the constitution of the Athletic Union, had been formally replaced by the recently-founded Association Football Club.[5] Cusack's proposals to introduce a different type of hurling therefore met with little or no opposition, and he seemed to go out of his way to draw into his circle members of the former Trinity club.

Having tested 'the pulse of the nation' by reviving hurling,

---

* These definitions were taken from the 1866 and then the 1867 rules of the Amateur Athletic Club in London.

and by initiating his own version of athletics, Cusack launched the Gaelic Athletic Association at Thurles on 1 November 1884. Among the small attendance were Maurice Davin, one of the country's leading athletes, and, piquantly enough, the local district inspector of the Royal Irish Constabulary, St George McCarthy, who had played rugby for Trinity and for Ireland, and had in fact played rugby against Cusack, for Trinity versus Phoenix, in the first Leinster Senior Cup tie, held at Lansdowne Road in December 1881.[6]

Cusack wanted the mechanic, the labourer and the artisan to play their full part in Irish sport. He intended to break with the sabbatarian tradition and arrange his matches and athletic meetings on the only day suitable for country people and the working class; further, he wished to break what he considered to be the Saxon stranglehold on Irish games.

The patrons of the GAA, Archbishop Croke of Cashel with Parnell* and Michael Davitt, represented Catholicism and nationalism, two forces with which the GAA was to become closely identified. At a meeting held in Thurles on 17 January 1885 (at which two of the ten participants represented the Nenagh Cricket Club and Literary Association), rules were drawn up for athletics, hurling, and football. It was proposed that a club should be founded in every parish, and resolved that 'after 17 March 1885 any athlete competing at meetings held under other laws than those of the GAA shall be ineligible for competing at any meeting held under the GAA.'[8] Thus the ban, which was soon to erect a partition between 'Gaelic' and 'foreign' games in Ireland, first emerged as a division in Irish athletics.

A riposte came within a week from R. J. Mecredy, the distinguished Trinity cyclist, at a meeting of the Irish Cycling Association. At this meeting Mecredy urged sportsmen to unite to quash the new Association, on the ground that it was a politically motivated body, pointing out that if Irish athletes competed under GAA rules, this would make them ineligible to compete in England.[9]

A meeting of athletes was hastily summoned in Dublin on 24 January 1885, at which a rival body, the Irish Amateur Athletic Association (IAAA) was formed. It was stressed that the GAA

* Earlier in his career Parnell had been a keen cricketer.[7]

did not represent Dublin or northern athletes, and it was agreed unanimously that 'the Gaelic Athletic Association does not command the confidence of Irish athletes, and that this meeting refuses to recognize the right of such an unrepresentative meeting [as that held in Thurles] to make laws governing athletics in Ireland'.[10]

Mecredy's reaction was typical of that of the great majority of Trinity sportsmen; but the obvious disapproval of one sector of the Irish sporting community had little effect on the explosive growth of the GAA, whose founders had rightly gauged the temper of the countryside, buoyed up by an improving economy and the rising tide of national feeling. Clubs were based on the parish, and representative structures on the county, thus encouraging the growth of local patriotism; and despite a bitter internecine struggle between the various shades of nationalism represented in the GAA–during which Cusack himself was ousted–clubs sprang up all over the country and affiliated to the association at an astonishing rate.

The first test of strength between the rival IAAA and the GAA took place on 17 June 1885, when the Co. Kerry Cricket and Athletic Club advertised an athletic meeting under IAAA rules to be held in Tralee. Cusack energetically organized a rival GAA meeting at a neighbouring venue, inviting Irish athletes to choose between 'Irish and foreign laws.' His efforts were vindicated by huge crowds, only a few hundred spectators turning up for the meeting held under the auspices of the IAAA.[11]

The GAA was already in a strong position when its first annual convention was held in October 1885. It had established itself widely throughout the country, was in the process of winning the hearts and minds of the majority of Irish athletes, and had codified the native games of hurling and football. In spite of protestations to the contrary, however, the association had become one of the bastions of emerging Irish nationalism, a political philosophy which few Trinity men of the time were able to endorse and one that within a short period was to lead to a complete division between those who participated in 'Gaelic' and in 'foreign' games.

Trinity had made a major contribution to Gaelic games by keeping a form of hurling alive when it was virtually extinct in the rest of the country. Trinity men were deeply involved in the tragic split in athletics (the precursor of the wider GAA ban) which occurred in 1885; happily the Dublin University Harriers and Athletic Club was just as deeply involved when that breach in Irish sport was eventually healed over eighty years later.

5

Postwar Revival

Athletic activities ground to a halt in Trinity during the First World War. Numbers dwindled by over a third as staff and students flocked to the colours.* Troops were quartered on the college grounds during the Easter Rising of 1916; sheep grazed in College Park; and the Officers' Training Corps commandeered the Gymnasium. 'An air of unreality prevails in every sphere of College life,' bemoaned the editor of *T.C.D.*,[1] who recalled in 1919 that 'the cricket ground became a meadow and the tennis courts ceased to exist; the boats remained unused at Islandbridge, and the Pavilion untenanted save by an occasional sentry'.[2]

Although a rapid return to normality was not to be expected on the cessation of hostilities, the clouds of gloom and despondency that had pervaded college life did not take long to lift. Most clubs had sprung to life by early 1919, and an *ad hoc* committee had been formed to assist in the rebirth of sport in the university. A request was made to the Board for the institution of a levy of one pound per student to support the clubs; this request was turned down in a letter from the Registrar indicating the decision that 'a Central Committee be formed consisting of the members of the existing Committee together with Prof. [W. E.] Thrift and Messrs. R. M. Gwynn and H. Thrift to reconstitute the athletic clubs, to take charge of the Pavilion and to report to the Board.'[3]

Thus DUCAC, the Dublin University Central Athletic Committee, was born, and a draft constitution stipulated that its membership should consist of four representatives from each of

---

* Almost 3000 Trinity men volunteered (there was no conscription in Ireland); 454 were killed. One of the fatalities occurred in Dublin: F. H. Browning, who had played rugby and cricket for Ireland and was president of the IRFU, was senior officer in the Irish Rugby Football Union Corps, one of four companies making up a body of unarmed veterans ambushed returning to Dublin after a route march on Easter Monday, 1916.

the Football, Cricket, Hockey and Boat Clubs, with two representatives from each of the Tennis, Association Football, Boxing and Gymnastic, Harriers and Athletic, Cycling, Golf and Swimming Clubs.* One representative from each club was to be of M. A. standing, and there were to be three representatives of the Board, one of whom was to be chairman.[4] W. E. Thrift, formerly an outstanding cyclist, was professor of natural and experimental philosophy and a representative of the junior fellows on the Board. He was later to become Provost, and was elected chairman at the first meeting of DUCAC.† His brother Harry, who had been observed in a race in College Park by Joyce's Leopold Bloom on his peregrination around Dublin,‡ was a mathematician who had won great distinction as a sprinter and an Irish wing-threequarter and rugby administrator (he was secretary of the International Rugby Football Board from 1933 to 1956); while R. M. Gwynn, professor of biblical Greek, was a distinguished rugby player, had played cricket for Ireland, and was noted for his social work on behalf of the Dublin poor.

The committee wasted no time in settling down to its task. An initial grant of £100 was obtained from the Board 'towards putting the Park in order,'[6] and a system of financial control was drawn up, a clause being inserted in the constitution at the Board's insistence: 'That the DUCAC account be not overdrawn without the permission of the Bursar.'[7] Although the individual clubs were to manage their own affairs, gate money and subscriptions were to be paid into a central fund, which would be used to pay ground staff, provide modest sums for the clubs, and defray expenses of teams in representative or intervarsity matches. A Pavilion and Grounds Subcommittee was established to under-

* As the popularity of the College Races declined from its peak in 1878, so did the income and kudos of the Athletic Union, which by the turn of the century gave small grants to clubs, administered the Pavilion, and organized the races.

† Like his predecessor Fitzgerald, W. E. Thrift was no disciplinarian, and his physics lectures, especially to engineering students, sometimes got out of hand. In the interests of law and order Harry Thrift would then sit through his brother's lectures, reading the *Irish Times*.

‡ The action of Joyce's novel *Ulysses* takes place on a single day, 16 June 1904, which happened to be the date of a sports meeting run jointly by the Bicycle and Harriers Clubs, a 'pleasant sequel' to the College Races held one week previously. The meeting consisted of four cycle races, three foot races and a composite race, and the events described by Joyce were the half-mile handicap cycle race and the quarter-mile foot race, in which Thrift was placed second.[5]

take the maintenance of these premises; and a second subvention of £320 was granted by the Board to compensate for the damage to sports facilities resulting from the military occupation of the college during the Easter Rising.[8]

In spite of the support given by the Board, which was a tribute to the wisdom of the authorities in acknowledging the importance of sporting activity in the life of the college, it was clear that further sources of finance must be forthcoming if the postwar clubs were to be established on a sound footing; and in May 1919 the following letter, which is worth quoting at some length, appeared in the press:

During the period of the War the activities of all athletic clubs in the University were suspended, as practically every student who was eligible joined one or other of His Majesty's Forces, and very few new students entered College.

We believe that all members of the University will agree that athletics form a most important part of College life and education, and that the splendid achievements of members of the College athletic clubs in the War were, in a large measure, due to the training they received in the various clubs.

At the beginning of the year a Committee was formed for the purpose of re-starting and re-organising the College athletic clubs, and if possible, placing them on a sounder basis than they were on before the War. The Committee has since been merged into a new body called the Dublin University Central Athletic Committee, representative of all the College clubs, and while each club will deal with its own special affairs, this Committee will undertake the management of College athletics generally.

The existing Pavilion in the College Park is being painted and re-paired, and the work of putting the grounds in order is being proceeded with as rapidly as possible.

In order to provide opportunities for past Trinity men to meet one another, and to maintain their interest in, and connection with the University, the Dublin University Central Athletic Committee has adopted the following resolution, which has received the approval of the Board of Trinity College:

'That all Fellows and Professors, and all graduates of the University and of Oxford and Cambridge Universities, be eligible for Pavilion Membership of all the College clubs, on payment of an annual subscription of one guinea ... '[9]

The scheme was an instant success (the Board ruled that Pavilion membership should be open to women[10]), and by the time of the first annual meeting in October, a sum of £379 (in a total income of £1,085) had accrued from this source, almost matching the initial Board subvention.[11]

The committee, under the chairmanship of W. E. Thrift, had to tread cautiously, as many of its resolutions required Board approval. Although these proposals were often modified in correspondence that shuttled to and fro between the secretary of DUCAC and the Registrar (as secretary to the Board), remarkably few of them were flatly turned down. This was a measure of the political skill and tact of the Board representatives on DUCAC (W. E. Thrift was a university representative in Dáil Eireann), as well as a further indication of the importance attached to properly organized athletic activities by the Board.

Goalposts were purchased for College Park, along with railings for the rugby ground. A water-ballast roller and top-dressing were acquired for the cricket square, and a telephone was installed in the Pavilion.[12] The first postwar away fixture was a visit by the Cricket Club to play Cork County at the Mardyke in July 1919; but when in December the Hockey Club applied for a grant to tour Cork and Waterford, it was resolved that 'while prepared to consider an application for a cross-channel tour versus Oxford and Cambridge, the Committee do not see their way to accede to the DUHC request for expenses to Cork and Waterford'.[13] The Hockey Club seized their opportunity, and early in 1920 embarked on a tour of Oxford and Cambridge.

As numbers in college and club activities increased, the necessity of providing extra playing-fields became apparent. With further Board support a ground was rented at Terenure, and the Board acceded to one of the many requests from the Boat Club for a subvention towards the repayments of the debentures and the mortgage on the club premises.[14] Some further financial underpinning of college sport was still necessary, and in June 1920 the Board sanctioned an annual grant of £1000 to DUCAC, provided the number of students on the books exceeded one thousand (the grant to be reduced proportionately if the number were less). The condition attached to the grant was that DUCAC would accept financial responsibility for all the men's and women's clubs.[15] Perhaps it was the necessity for the Board to find such a large annual subvention that prompted the view of Provost Bernard (formerly an enthusiastic member of the Hurley Club) that a sports levy should be imposed on every student 'as in other universities and places of useful learning'.[16]

Trinity Week, the festival of sporting and social activity that had grown up around the College Races at the end of Trinity Term, was revived in 1920. The programme included a two-day cricket match, the university tennis and boxing championships, a Choral Society concert, and the College Races, as well as an intervarsity sports on the final Saturday, preceded by the Trinity Ball on the Friday evening.

For some time it had been clear that the changing accommodation in the Pavilion (which then consisted of the central block of the present building) was inadequate, and that hot water should be installed. The original building may have met with the Board's aesthetic approval, but from a utilitarian point of view it left much to be desired. ('Whoever was architect of that atrocious structure', J. G. Cronyn, one of the early rugby men, remarked to Watson, 'was hampered in his design by Traill! At least that was the general impression.'[17]) A plan had been formulated before the war to build a new pavilion on the western side of the park, and a sum of £500 had been subscribed for that purpose.[18]* But costs had escalated, and in May 1920 it was agreed, with the approval of the subscribers and the Board, to add a wing to the north of the existing Pavilion, at a cost of £720.[19] In 1933, when the construction of a bath-house in Botany Bay was under consideration, the Board granted £100 on the understanding that DUCAC would find the balance necessary to install hot water, to improve the showers and toilets in the Pavilion, and to carry out some necessary repairs to the boathouse at Islandbridge.[20]

The fledgling committee had to face a crisis, not of its own making, during the Anglo-Irish conflict of 1921. Six Trinity men were playing cricket for the Gentlemen of Ireland versus the Military in College Park on 3 June when a gunman opened fire through the railings along Nassau Street. A woman spectator (an undergraduate) was killed, but the players escaped injury by throwing themselves to the ground. After a threatening letter had been received, the chairman, in consultation with the Provost, cancelled the arrangements for Trinity Week,[21] and the joint treasurers, in the autumn, reported to the committee that 'owing to the very unsettled state of the country, receipts from gates,

---

* The appeal was (nominally) spearheaded by Sir Edward Carson, who represented the university in Parliament from 1892 to 1918 and had played hurley as a Trinity undergraduate.

especially in the case of matches with cross-channel teams, are an uncertain item.'[22] The annual general meeting of 1922 had to be postponed on account of the disturbances, a civil war having followed the signing of the Anglo-Irish Treaty,[23] and only a truncated version of Trinity Week was held in 1923.[24]

The First World War marked, in more than one sense, the end of an epoch for Trinity, for when conditions again became settled, a constitutional revolution had taken place, and the college found itself in a partitioned Ireland outside the United Kingdom. Faced with the prospect of divided loyalties, it was not at all clear how the university's relationship with the Free State would develop.* Moreover, at a time when British universities were growing in strength and prestige, Trinity found itself lacking in the resources necessary to meet the challenges posed by a changing world.

The financial problems that had been mounting in these troubled times reached crisis point in 1924, when two groundsmen were let go and overtime was prohibited.[26] An 'all-night' dance held in December produced only the meagre return of £25,[27] and inevitably an approach was made to the college. The Board agreed to make four annual payments to DUCAC; to share equally the burden of the wages of the ground staff and the cost of machinery; and to take over responsibility for pensions. The *quid pro quo*, which was readily accepted, was the appointment of Captain J. H. Shaw, a college official, as treasurer of DUCAC.[28] Thus began Jimmy Shaw's thirty-five years of loyal and efficient service to sport in Trinity. The unconventional method of his appointment meant that when he eventually retired from office, no constitutional method existed for the appointment of a successor!

The Medical School, for a brief period in the early part of the century, offered a number of scholarships to students from South Africa. This led to an influx of Afrikaner undergraduates during the First World War (some of them Rhodes scholars), who might otherwise have studied at Oxford or Cambridge but came to Dublin to avoid conscription. The proud Boer rugby tradition proved an unexpected bonus to the Football Club, and with players such as Ivan Marais, an ebullient if diminutive full-back, D. J. Malan, a balding six-foot scrum-half, and Jan van Druten, arguably the finest forward to play in Ireland (he

* Rumours persisted during the postwar period of a scheme to build a roadway through the College Park.[25]

64

returned to South Africa to win Springbok honours), Trinity were the dominating force in postwar Irish rugby. The South African period lasted for four seasons after the war,* but the Boers were then succeeded by an equally talented group of Irish players: Denis Cussen, a flying wing-threequarter who, as a sprinter, became the first Irishman to break even time; the brothers Pike in the scrum; Mark Sugden, a scrum-half famous for his dummy who, although an Englishman, also played cricket for Ireland; and the incomparable Jammie Clinch. In an international against France, the referee was forced to intervene after an incident in which a Frenchman had lost a couple of teeth. He and Clinch were asked to shake hands; Jammie offered his hand with a wide grin and an apology that delighted his opponent: 'I'm sorry I didn't knock the whole bloody lot of them out!' Clinch's father had captained Trinity and played for Ireland; as a back-row forward he himself won thirty caps as well as a Lions tour to South Africa; his son captained DUFC; and his grandson Paul also captained the club. Four generations of the Clinch family have won colours for the Dublin University Football Club – a record unlikely to be equalled in any sport in any university.

In March 1925 the Pavilion Members Committee presented a design for a Trinity tie, consisting of red, green and light-blue stripes on a black background – the red and black representing the colours of the Football Club and the green and black the colours of the Hockey Club, with the blue of the college coat of arms.[29] This tie was not to be restricted to sportsmen and women, and the design was approved by both the main debating societies, the College Historical Society and the University Philosophical Society, as well as by the Board. In 1928 the TCD Association was formed by graduates, and it was agreed that the tie could be worn by Pavilion members of DUCAC as well as by members of the association.[30] Thus in a real sense both the graduates' association and its distinctive colours derive from the DUCAC scheme of Pavilion membership.

The minute-book covering the period 1919-26 ended with a flourish from the secretary, D. St Clair Mackenzie, 'Here endeth

* A team called the Trinity South Africans took part in an unofficial competition in the season 1918-19 with a number of other Dublin clubs. The competition was left undecided, Trinity and UCD having played two exciting drawn finals in College Park.

the first Minute Book of the Dublin University Central Athletic Committee.'[31] The committee had been established at a period of great uncertainty in the history of the college. It had overcome, with generous Board support, crises caused by guerrilla warfare and by financial disability, and had settled on a pattern of administration that was to prove durable in the decades ahead.

6

Consolidation

Two important proposals were put before the annual general meeting of DUCAC in 1926. A combined subscription of £2 was adopted, with an additional subscription of one shilling payable to the individual club; and pink was recommended as the university colour in a motion debated with much impassioned oratory.[1]

The choice of a university colour and the conditions for its award had been under discussion for some considerable time. Dark green and 'St Patrick's blue' (from the college coat of arms) had both been suggested, and the former had been settled on by the Athletic Union in 1895,[2] but nothing had come of this decision because of opposition from the clubs. On this occasion, however, both the colour and the scheme for its award were approved by the meeting.* Club colours were to be awarded in the individual sports as heretofore; pinks were to be awarded by DUCAC, not on team performance but for outstanding individual merit.

The matter was referred to higher authority, and word was received that 'the Board disapprove of pink,' though the regulations governing the award had been approved.[4] Nothing daunted, the secretary resubmitted the proposal to the Board, pointing out that DUCAC had approved the colour only after long discussion.[5] The Board appointed two members to discuss the problem with the committee, and on 30 May 1927 it was reported that:

the Board, while not wishing to veto the considered choice of the various athletic clubs of pink as a University Colour, feel that a decision so

---

* Legend has it that the honorary secretary–Terence Millin, an international threequarter who captained one of the university's strongest football sides (which adopted the unorthodox formation of seven forwards and eight backs) and later became a Harley Street surgeon–persuaded the committee on the ground that pink was the racing colour of the college's foundress, Queen Elizabeth I![3]

seriously affecting future generations of College men should not be carried immediately into effect. If therefore the DUCAC reaffirm in Trinity Term 1928, by a decision more or less unanimous, the choice of pink, the Board will offer no further objection.[6]

The choice of colour having been duly confirmed, the Captains' Committee (consisting of captains of the affiliated clubs) was set up to recommend candidate pinks to DUCAC, the parent body reserving the right of veto.[7]

Politics reared its head again in Trinity Week of 1929 with the refusal of the Governor-General of the Free State to attend the College Races, as proceedings ended with the playing of 'God Save the King'. Some of the athletic clubs outside the college took a similar view, putting their participation in jeopardy, but the Provost urged caution. He wished to ascertain whether the playing of 'God Save the King' was the real problem or whether, if that anthem were omitted, the unhappy visitors would insist on its replacement with 'The Soldier's Song'.[8]

The Hockey Club embarked on its golden era in the 1930s, winning the Irish Senior Cup for three consecutive years in 1934-36, with players such as Denis Coulson* (one of the finest centre-halves to play hockey), J. K. Craig (full-back), J. A. McDonogh (centre-forward) and George McVeagh, a quadruple international. These four players won seventy-one international caps between them in the period 1932-39, and McVeagh, from the left wing, captained an Irish eleven with a preponderance of Trinity men that won the Triple Crown in the three years 1937-39. McVeagh, who is Trinity's finest all-round sportsman, captained Ireland at squash, tennis, hockey, and cricket. He is perhaps best remembered for scoring an undefeated century and taking four second-innings catches in Ireland's thrilling victory over the West Indies at College Park in 1928.

A Ladies' Hockey Club had been formed in 1905 shortly after women were admitted to the college. The Board agreed to rent a playing-field at Ballsbridge,[9] and after a protracted struggle with their male counterparts the ladies were held entitled to wear the old Hurley Club colours of green and black. Trinity Hall in Dartry, purchased as a women's residence in 1908, provided a

---

* Coulson trained by dribbling the ball up the pitch holding the stick with one hand, then down the pitch with the other. The Irish Senior Cup returned to Trinity in 1942 and 1943. The university has won the trophy eleven times.

permanent home for the club for many years.

In 1929 the club protested that it should be represented on DUCAC by its own members rather than by members of the men's club.[10] It was some years before this nettle would be grasped, for a similar proposal was turned down as late as 1941, when it was resolved that representatives of the ladies' clubs could put their cases to Captain Shaw, who would then relay them to the committee.[11]

Three sports clubs dating from this era have long associations with the university without being formally affiliated to DUCAC. Dublin University Motor Cycle and Light Car Club was founded in 1923 with John Joly—the distinguished physicist and professor of geology, inventor of colour photography, pioneer motor-cyclist, and proud possessor of a flat twin Harley-Davidson—as president. The club recruits Trinity students and graduates as members but does not confine itself exclusively to them; the TT winner Stanley Woods competed for the club for a number of years, although not a Trinity man. In recent times the club (now reconstituted as a limited company) has confined itself exclusively to car rallying, and in Paddy Hopkirk (winner of the Monte Carlo rally in 1964) and Benny Crawford has produced two of Ireland's outstanding rally drivers.[12]

The membership of Dublin University Golfing Society is confined to Trinity men, the great majority of whom are former members of the Golf Club. The society was founded in 1909 under the chairmanship of Provost Traill, but it lapsed through inactivity, to be revived in 1926 under the presidency of Harry Thrift. The society has arranged a number of highly successful fixtures with the Oxford and Cambridge Golfing Society, and an admirable tradition has evolved of a graduate match against UCD that takes place on the day of the annual Colours Match between the university golf clubs at Portmarnock. The society plays a valuable role in cementing comradeships formed, initially, in the university club and in giving much-needed fiscal and indeed moral support to Trinity's student golfers.[13]

The third club, whose origins date back to the turn of the century, is somewhat more difficult to pin down, for although membership of the Lady Elizabeth Boat Club is confined to former members of the University Boat Club, and it has occasionally put crews on the water (even at Henley), its exact relationship with

DUBC has never been satisfactorily spelt out. The Lady Elizabeth does provide welcome and substantial assistance to the harassed treasurer of DUBC, and when thorny constitutional questions arise, these tend, Boat Club aficionados claim, to be dissolved in a sea of stout!

By 1936 a revitalized Hurling Club,* a Ladies' Swimming Club and a Lacrosse Club had affiliated to DUCAC. The first lacrosse match in Ireland, which attracted immense publicity, had been played on 10 May 1876 at the North of Ireland Cricket Club, Belfast, by a Canadian team against a team of Iroquois Indians.[14] The Indians, who appeared in head-dress and warpaint, included players with such colourful names as Hickory Woodsplit, Hole in the Sky, Great Arm, and Wild Wind. Three days later the two teams played again, this time before the Lord Lieutenant at the ICAC, Lansdowne Road.[15] A Lacrosse Club was subsequently formed in Trinity, with the inevitable Dr Traill as president, and an Irish Lacrosse Union founded. The club did not last long, but was revived as a ladies' club in 1936, and survived until the 1970s. Its final years were marked by an annual match against the Knights of the Campanile in the College Park.

A Squash Club, too, was proposed in 1936, with the attendant problem of constructing courts; and the possibility of building a stand beside the rugby ground was mooted. In 1927 the bank along the ground's northern touchline had been extended with material excavated during the erection of the Hall of Honour (a war memorial in the Front Square, to which a reading room was later added). In 1931 a press box was put up on the bank for the modest sum, even for those carefree days, of £20.[16] The Board was asked in 1937 to lend the sum of £1400 for the construction of three squash courts abutting onto the Gymnasium, and agreed, subject to an annual repayment by DUCAC of £100. The Board also agreed to lend £700 at 3 per cent (to be repaid over seven years) towards the erection of a stand.[17]

Shortly after this, W. E. Thrift, the first chairman of DUCAC, was appointed Provost. He was succeeded as chairman by his brother Harry, who promptly became Bursar, further strengthening DUCAC's hand in the upper echelons of the college. The Board then approved the plans which had been drawn up for

---

* The Hurling Club was later to suffer yet another lapse before undergoing an effective revival in the 1960s.

the stand and increased the loan to £1000.[18] The Football Club calculated that the extra gate money would amply cover repayments on the stand, but prohibitive cost increases following the outbreak of the Second World War impeded the plan, which never came to fruition.[19]

The awarding of pinks by the Captains' Committee set up in 1928 had not proved a harmonious arrangement. A recommendation from that committee that the practice be discontinued was made to DUCAC in 1936.[20] The inevitable subcommittee that was established to deliberate upon the problem came to a similar conclusion, reporting that it could ascertain no objective grounds on which pinks should be awarded. A DUCAC motion giving effect to this recommendation was passed by 28 votes to 4 with 6 abstentions,[21] and the practice of awarding pinks went into abeyance, only to be resuscitated five years later.

In May 1943 the women's clubs were at last permitted to nominate their own representatives to DUCAC. It had been a lengthy struggle, and the chairman congratulated them on achieving their objective. He confessed that 'he never for one moment feared that they would be unable to carry out their duties and be fit representatives, but what had always been the fear in the past was that maybe one year their representatives would be good, but next year they might be so timid that they would not be able to defend their cause ... ' The women's representatives did not reply, the minutes record, but 'it seemed by their expressions that satisfaction was felt by them.'[22]

In June of that year a problem arose concerning the Knights of the Campanile.[23] The Knights, who constitute not so much a club as a society of hospitable sportsmen with an elected membership, had been set up in 1926 to entertain visiting teams, particularly those from Oxford and Cambridge. In this they fulfil the role played by Vincent's Club in Oxford and the Hawks Club in Cambridge. The Knights' tie reflects this connection, with dark blue representing Oxford, a blueish silver for Cambridge, and a tinge of pink for Trinity. The Knights' problems generally fall into one of two categories: overenthusiastic hospitality, or underenthusiastic accounting. They now receive a modest subvention from DUCAC, and have taken on the extra responsibility of defraying the costs incurred by individual Trinity sportsmen in representative fixtures.*

At one annual meeting of the Knights the treasurer, F. B. V. Keane, a fine scrum-half who captained the Football Club, was having difficulty in unravelling the expenditure side of his accounts. When pressed on an unattributed item he surprised the meeting, and regained the initiative, by asking the assembled Knights to rise and pay a silent tribute to a recently deceased member of the society, the debit under consideration being the cost of the wreath. When the members had resumed their seats the meeting was brought to an uproarious conclusion with the observation that the silent tribute had been paid to the florist![†]

At the annual meeting of DUCAC in 1944 T. R. B. Taylor was elected honorary secretary of the Pavilion and Grounds Subcommittee. Before allowing his name to be put forward, Taylor had sensibly enquired about his duties, but, as Raymond Oliver, the highly articulate secretary of DUCAC, reported, 'no-one knew what these were or whether the office existed. Eventually Mr Taylor, with unflinching courage, accepted the burden of his unknown duties in the apparent hope that they would not be discovered.'[24]

Not long afterwards the finances of the Golf Club came under committee scrutiny. It was revealed that by paying the subscription of ten shillings, members apparently became entitled 'to play at a reduced fee on certain Dublin golf-courses; to tour to Cork; to stand professionals drinks; to entertain various teams to luncheons, teas, suppers and dinners; and to pay the green fees of all and sundry–all at the expense of DUCAC.' A suggestion that the subscription be increased was approved by all present, including the Golf Club's exhausted treasurer![25]

The awarding of pinks had been revived in 1941 on the basis that anyone who had been awarded senior club colours would be entitled to sport a pink.[26] Six years later, with five women's clubs–Hockey, Swimming, Lacrosse, Cricket, and Athletics–affiliated to DUCAC, the problem of awarding pinks to women was discussed by the committee.[27] No conclusion was reached,

* The Hereans, a women's society, has recently been formed as a counterpart to the Knights of the Campanile. Hera was the wife of Zeus, and the Herean Games at Argos included foot-races for female virgins.

† Frankie Kerr, celebrated Boxing Club coach and the Knight to whom tribute should have been paid, must have enjoyed the incident from a safe vantage point.

and six months later it was proposed that the practice of awarding university colours be abandoned, and that there should at least be a change from the hideous colour pink.[28] An unsatisfactory compromise was reached in 1950 by which a certain number of pinks were to be awarded annually, fixed numbers being allotted to individual clubs. The schedule that was drawn up, not without some contention, read as follows: 'Football 8, Cricket 6, Hockey 6, Boat 5, Harriers and Athletics 3, with Boxing, Association Football, Squash and Swimming, 2 each.' A rider was added by which no pink was to be awarded to a member of the Sailing Club unless exceptional merit were shown![29]

An arrangement such as this was bound to lead to problems, one of which was forcefully expressed by Miss Huet, captain of the Ladies' Swimming Club, in October 1952, when pinks were awarded to two members of the Sailing Club. She enquired if, now that the Sailing Club had lady members, they were eligible for pinks? The club representative replied that he thought not. Miss Huet, sticking to her guns, demanded pinks for women, and uproar followed.[30] One month later the Captains' Committee* recommended awards to women by 7 votes to 6; this recommendation was endorsed by DUCAC by 11 votes to 8, and another bastion of male supremacy had been swept aside.[31]†

The years after the Second World War were gloomy ones for Ireland, with stagnation in cultural, political and economic affairs leading to emigration at record levels. Life south of the border was disfigured by a series of anachronistic institutionalized restraints including censorship, the prohibition of divorce and of 'artificial' methods of family planning, the ban on Catholic students attending Trinity, the GAA ban, and the restriction of women's athletics, while in the north it was affected by sectarian division. In the public perception, Trinity and UCD represented opposite poles of the socio-religious spectrum in Ireland, and the developing sporting contacts between the two colleges, which were then considerably stronger than those on the academic

---

* Canon R. R. Hartford, Regius Professor of Divinity, was chairman of the Trinity Week Committee, the Captains' Committee and the Pavilion and Grounds Subcommittee in the 1950s.

† Joyce Lavan (Squash Club) was the first woman to be awarded a pink, while a member of the same team, Gilda Horsley, who was English, became the first Trinity woman to play squash for Ireland.

plane, achieved a significance, accordingly, that extended way beyond the sporting arena.

A far-reaching change in the Football Club's fixture list occurred in 1952. Up to that time football colours had been awarded to members of the side that played in the annual game at home against either Oxford or Cambridge. Since 1919 UCD had been a senior club, and many stirring encounters between the two Dublin colleges had taken place in the Leinster Cup. Early in the series Trinity, with its South African contingent, had held the upper hand, but by the 1940s the pendulum had swung in favour of UCD. These matches were always particularly keenly contested, and in 1948 the two universities met in the final of the Leinster Cup. In a memorable match before a record crowd, UCD triumphed by a dropped goal to nil. It was this game, and the great public interest generated, that led Harry Thrift, representing DUFC, and Sarsfield Hogan of UCD (both of whom served as Irish delegates on the International Rugby Football Board from 1946 to 1956) to canvass the idea of an annual intervarsity match in Dublin on the basis of which each club would award its colours. The first such fixture took place in Lansdowne Road in 1952, and the annual Colours Match between the two clubs now holds an important place in the Irish rugby calendar.

The two university clubs had combined to play against the Rest of Leinster in College Park as early as January 1921. Other events that brought them closer together were the fielding of a Combined Universities of Ireland Fifteen, whose first fixture took place against an International Fifteen at Lansdowne Road in 1933; and the formation of the Irish Universities Rugby Union in 1950-51, whose first president, Air Vice-Marshal Sir William Tyrrell, was a distinguished Queen's University man and the then president of the IRFU.

In another sporting context in the 1960s the combined forces of Trinity and UCD were to make a significant impact on the changing Irish scene. The deep divisions between sportsmen and women that had become apparent with the foundation of the GAA, mirroring even deeper divisions in Irish society, had had their origin in a dispute over the administration of athletics. This had led to a situation in which it was impossible for participants in what were regarded as the Gaelic games (Gaelic football, hurling, handball, and camogie*) to play the so-called 'foreign' games (rugby, soccer, hockey, and cricket) and vice versa. The 'ban' also extended to athletics, but the two athletic bodies, one associated with and the other opposed to the GAA, had learned to co-exist, and after the establishment of the Free State in 1922 came together to form the National Athletics and Cycling Association of Ireland (NACAI), which catered for athletes in the whole country. The NACAI was recognized in 1924 by the International Amateur Athletic Federation (IAAF), which had been set up in 1912; but the unity which had thus been established was paper-thin, and in 1925 a group of Belfast clubs broke away from the NACAI, appealing for support to the Amateur Athletic Association in Britain.

Attempts were made to find a remedy, but to no avail; and the problem was exacerbated in 1934, when the IAAF decreed that the jurisdiction of affiliated bodies be delimited by the political boundaries of the states they represented. The NACAI refused to accept this ruling, arguing that it represented athletes in both parts of Ireland. This led to a rupture with the IAAF by which Ireland was effectively excluded from international competitions, including the Olympic Games,[†] in which Irish athletes had featured prominently since 1896.

Further rifts then occurred north and south of the border, turning the administrative structure of Irish athletics into a veritable labyrinth. The Amateur Athletic Union of Eire (AAUE) was formed by clubs in the south that broke away from the NACAI, including Dublin University Harriers and Athletic Club; and an equivalent body, the Northern Ireland Amateur Athletics Association (NIAAA), was established across the border. The AAUE was now recognized by the IAAF as the controlling body for athletes in the south of Ireland. The AAUE and the NIAAA combined to hold Irish championships and to select a joint Irish team for the home internationals, but the final result was a dichotomy in Irish athletics, with NACAI athletes unable to compete with colleagues whose clubs were affiliated either to the AAUE or to the NIAAA.

The situation cried out for redress, but a number of attempts

---

* Women's hurling.

† D. D. Bulger was one of the two IAAA delegates to attend the Paris meeting of 1894 which founded the International Olympic Committee.

to hammer out a compromise ended in failure. By 1960 the two universities in Dublin dominated competition in their rival associations. Trinity, with Colin Shillington at 880 yards, Bob Francis at 220 and 440, and Tjerund Lunde from Norway outstanding at jumping, throwing and sprinting, reigned supreme in the AAUE, while their opposite numbers at UCD held a similar position of strength in the NACAI.

Athletics coach Cyril White, aided by George Dawson, a fellow in genetics who was for many years chairman of the Captains' Committee of DUCAC, worked cautiously behind the scenes to break the mould, while similar efforts were made by P. C. Moore, Judge J. C. Conroy, Fionnbar Callanan and athletics coach Jack Sweeney in UCD. Francis Quinlan, Trinity Athletics secretary, and Tony Sparshott, his opposite number in the Harriers, attended a series of meetings of the AAUE during the winter of 1960-61, chaired by Jim Moran, a former Trinity athlete, at which permission was eventually granted for Trinity to participate in a 'closed' competition with UCD.

Inspiration had come from the United States, where universities had gained considerable autonomy in intercollegiate athletic affairs. The first authorized Trinity v. UCD athletics match for twenty-five years, attracting intense interest and three thousand spectators, took place in College Park in June 1961.* This led inevitably to the institution of an annual intervarsity athletic competition in which all Irish universities could participate. Ultimately, in 1967, Bord Lúthchleas na hEireann (BLE) took over from the AAUE and the NACAI to become the internationally recognized body representing all athletes in the Republic, with the NIAAA acting as a regional athletics board for Northern Ireland. It was particularly fitting that Trinity, which had been involved in the earlier division, should have been an active participant, with UCD, in the first successful move to heal the rift in Irish athletics.[†]

An unexpected bonus for the Golf Club came in 1953 in the

---

* An unauthorized athletics match between the two colleges held in 1953 had caused considerable fluttering in official dovecotes.

† The GAA ban prohibiting members of the association from playing in, or watching, 'foreign' games was formally revoked in 1971. Given the links, in 1885, of the Protestant athletic establishment with unionism and of the GAA with nationalism, some such dichotomy was probably inevitable; the tragedy is that the ban so long outlasted the conditions that gave rise to it.

form of a £500 bequest from the parents of Archie Taylor, a former captain who had died within a few years of graduation. The principal was invested, and the interest designated to offset expenses of competitors in the annual Boyd Quaich international university competition held on the Old Course at St Andrews.[32] The Quaich, a shallow silver bowl with two handles, had been presented by the parents of two brothers, both students at St Andrews University, who were killed in the second world war. A Trinity golfer, J. L. Bamford, won the trophy in 1954, posting a record score of 290 for four rounds, and repeated his triumph two years later.

The Golf Club's finances came under further baleful scrutiny in 1954, when a request for travel expenses for the Murphy Cup match, the annual colours match against UCD held at Royal Dublin, less than three miles from the college, was turned down with the observation that an application for such travel expenses indicated 'a low estimate of the perspicacity of DUCAC'.[33] A complaint had arisen some years previously concerning UCD's practice of fielding graduates in their colours teams. This practice had in fact been welcomed by a Boat Club representative on the ground that the older the crew was, the slower it went![34]

No Trinity golfer of the modern era has approached Lionel Munn's stature, but prominent Irish internationals include H. A. Boyd, J. F. Jameson, A. W. Briscoe, J. R. Mahon and J. L. Bamford. More recently R. K. M. Polin won the West of Ireland Championship twice as an undergraduate in 1967 and 1969, and the Irish Close Championship in 1973, while Arthur Pierse has joined Munn as a Trinity golfer selected to represent Britain and Ireland in the Walker Cup.

A bombshell at the 1953 annual general meeting was the proffered resignation of the treasurer, Captain Shaw, after thirty years in office. He was persuaded to postpone his retirement after he himself had adverted to the fact that, as he was a Board appointee, the DUCAC constitution laid down no guidelines for the appointment of a successor.[35]

On a more sombre note, a request for a contribution towards a pension for the widow of a groundsman, Albert Fitzgerald, who had died after thirty-three years' service, was rejected. The secretary was, however, authorized to arrange a collection for the widow among members of the clubs.[36] Fitzgerald had served on the Essex ground staff, and then in the First World War, coming to Trinity on demobilization. After his death the cricket square deteriorated, for it is well-nigh impossible in Ireland to employ ground staff skilled in the preparation and maintenance of cricket pitches.

The Gaelic Football Club was affiliated to DUCAC in March 1954.[37] Pinks were awarded at an extraordinary meeting three months later to two distinguished members of the club, Kevin Heffernan and Colm Kennelly, who had won All-Ireland medals with Dublin and Kerry respectively.[38] Heffernan was to achieve further distinction in 1976 as coach to a Dublin team (captained by another Trinity man, Tony Hanahoe) that won the All-Ireland championship, and again in 1986 as manager of a successful Irish team that played a series of games under a composite code against Rules footballers in Australia. In 1988 Heffernan was conferred with an honorary doctorate at the special commencements to mark Dublin's millennium, in recognition of his contribution to sport in the city, while the Kennelly connection with the college is maintained by the footballer's younger brother Brendan, a fellow and a poet and playwright of international repute.

An alteration in the financial relationship between the Central Committee and the clubs, with far-reaching implications, was passed, after due deliberation, in 1954. Heretofore grants had been made to clubs on the basis of detailed applications for individual items of equipment, travel expenses, entertainment, and so on, which were scrutinized by a Financial Subcommittee responsible for making recommendations to DUCAC. In future, it was decided, clubs should submit an annual budget to DUCAC at the beginning of each academic year in respect of current expenditure, and would receive a single lump-sum allocation. Requests for capital expenditure, for example on boats, would be dealt with separately.[39] This system, satisfactory in theory, broke down in practice, and the committee reverted after only one year to the policy of grant applications per item, taking into account club expenditure over previous years.[40] It is this system that prevails at present, giving the committee – its officials boast – much tighter control over its hard-won revenues.

Another important proposal that surfaced, not for the first time, was for the imposition of a sports levy on every student. This would then provide the bulk of DUCAC's income, allowing club subscriptions to be reduced to a nominal level. In January 1955 a DUCAC deputation waited on the Provost (Dr A. J. McConnell), who did not reject the proposal but suggested that if the college societies were included it would considerably strengthen the chances of acceptance.[41] A capitation levy for clubs and societies was introduced by the Board in 1957.

At the annual general meeting of 1956 at which this financial innovation was announced, Harry Thrift (who had succeeded his brother as chairman in 1937) announced his resignation on the ground of ill health.[42] The Thrift brothers had, between them, guided the fortunes of DUCAC for thirty-seven years, and had made an immense contribution both to the playing and to the administration of sport in the university.

7

Expansion

John Luce, who succeeded to the chairmanship on Harry Thrift's retirement, was to preside over DUCAC for two decades, thus maintaining the tradition of long service established by his predecessors. A classicist, and a distinguished hockey player who had captained the university in hockey, cricket and squash, his best years came during the Second World War; thereafter he won six caps on the left wing for Ireland. His father, Arthur Aston Luce, a First World War veteran, philosopher and fisherman, who was a fellow for sixty-five years, had served on the committee before him.

Although it was not at all apparent in 1956, the twenty years of Luce's chairmanship were to witness some of the more dramatic developments in the 400-year history of the university. In 1956 Trinity had 2500 students; twenty years later that number had trebled. The ban on Catholic students attending Trinity was still in place in 1956, although its effect was lessening, and the student body contained a high proportion of Englishmen and women, and many Ulster students, almost all from one side of the religio-political divide. Twenty years later the composition of the student body more accurately mirrored the religious and political spectrum of the whole country.*

The imposition of the capitation fee, for which DUCAC had been arguing since its foundation, afforded the committee a real opportunity for future planning. The funds accruing from the levy were divided up by the Standing Committee of Clubs

* The situation had changed so markedly by the late 1960s, with large numbers of applicants for university places, that the government, in a move designed to control expenditure, proposed a merger between Trinity and UCD. By this time UCD was concentrated at Belfield, a couple of miles south of its former city-centre site, so the logic behind the merger was questionable. It was eventually resisted by the two colleges, but led to some rationalization of faculties.

and Societies (now the Capitation Committee), presided over by the Senior Dean (in 1957, F. La Touche Godfrey). Before an application for funds was entertained, DUCAC's audited accounts were scrutinized by this committee. The capitation fund provided DUCAC with a stable financial base, but new and improved facilities were needed for the increasing numbers of students and of clubs. It was clear that a development fund would be necessary if capital projects such as the provision of new pitches, changing rooms, or indoor facilities, were ever to be brought to fruition.

The administration of the Central Committee would also have to be streamlined to deal with extra clubs and participants. In October 1957 the Knights of the Campanile made a related request to DUCAC. Might the society be granted a permanent base that could be used to further the social side of sport in the college?[1] Provost McConnell, a Knight himself, was not unsympathetic, and DUCAC, and the Knights, were allocated permanent rooms on the top floor of no. 27, TCD.

As a first step towards the provision of new facilities, the Pavilion in College Park was extended (with the aid of a grant from the Trinity Trust) by addition of a southern wing containing extra changing-rooms, thus restoring the symmetry of the original building. Plans were put forward for extra pitches to be laid in the grounds of Trinity Hall (the student residence some distance south of the college), but not enough space was available. The possibility of obtaining pitches on the Royal Dublin Society's grounds at Simmonscourt was discussed; and in 1959 the Board proposed to earmark a proportion of the college's botanic gardens at Lansdowne Road for sports grounds.[2] Six months later this proposal was withdrawn 'for an urgent and important reason',[3] and in March 1960 the Board sold the botanic gardens as a hotel site, promising to provide sports grounds north of the Liffey, where land was cheaper.[4] The following October, thirty-four acres were purchased for £10,000 at Santry, three miles north of the college.[5] These grounds now contain two all-weather hockey pitches, two rugby pitches, two soccer pitches, a Gaelic pitch, and a camogie pitch. A pavilion was erected, the necessary sum being borrowed from the college on the strength of the surplus in the capitation fund, and in 1969 the pavilion was doubled in size, under a similar arrangement. The Santry site also contains a large book repository, which acts as an overflow for the college's copyright library.

The Hockey Club, with one pitch in College Park, had travelled around the city in search of a second, playing at various times in Palmerston Park, Anglesea Road, Kenilworth Park, Park Avenue and Londonbridge Road, finally settling in its second home at Santry. Forwards of the calibre of W. E. Haughton (an inside-forward with a ferocious shot), R. B. Fitzsimon and J. N. Lavan; mid-fielders such as K. G. Blackmore, S. McNulty and J. Douglas; and defenders as experienced as D. Judge (with over a century of caps) and I. Steepe, are Trinity men of the period after the Second World War who have made an immense contribution to Irish hockey.

The Board in 1950 had assumed responsibility for the maintenance of the college sports grounds, as well as giving an annual grant to DUCAC. This grant ceased with the introduction of the capitation fee in 1957, but in 1959 the Board announced that it was going to require a sum of £1,000 annually towards general maintenance from DUCAC's revenue. The secretary was instructed to write a vigorous letter to the Board opposing this scheme.[6] Agreement was eventually reached that the college should cover three-quarters of the cost of maintaining Santry, and put £3000 annually towards the running of College Park, with DUCAC making up the balance.[7]

A more general arrangement was reached in 1970 which involved societies as well as clubs. The capitation fee in that year stood at £9, and it was agreed that for the next year, and in future, the capitation fee would decrease by £2, while the tuition fee would increase by the same amount; the composite fee thus remaining the same for every student. This transfer of £2 out of the capitation fee was made on the basis that the college would take on full responsibility for providing the following services:

(1) the cleaning of societies' rooms;
(2) the redecoration of premises of clubs and societies, to be carried out every five years;
(3) the maintenance of the playing fields, pavilions and boathouse;
(4) the heating and lighting of the premises of clubs and societies.[8]

In 1959 Barry Brewster, the energetic secretary of Trinity Week, proposed that the Trinity Ball–which, in common with the other activities of Trinity Week, was organized by DUCAC, and was currently held in two Dublin hotels–should be run in college.[9] This proposal was enthusiastically supported by the student body, and was approved by the Board, though only (so the story goes) by the narrowest of margins.[10] Since 1960 the ball has been held in college, with dancing in the Dining and Examination Halls and in a marquee. Although the organization of the ball (which is no longer the responsibility of DUCAC) is fraught with difficulty, causing considerable disruption at the beginning of examinations in May, its popularity in the Trinity and Dublin social calendar is undisputed. It provides a glamorous, if necessarily hectic, finale to the teaching weeks of the Trinity term.

The development of women's athletics south of the border in the postwar period forms an eccentric codicil to the convoluted legacy left by their male counterparts. Little competition had been arranged for women athletes before the Second World War, although there had been an occasional event in the College Races; but in 1948 activity on this front received a stimulus from the achievement of the Dutch athlete, Fanny Blankers-Koen, in winning four gold medals in the sprint events at the London Olympics. Mrs Blankers-Koen then ran at a meeting in Lansdowne Road, but the emergence of women's athletics in the south of Ireland was nipped smartly in the bud by the Catholic archbishop of Dublin.

Dr John Charles McQuaid was a conservative churchman who rarely missed the opportunity offered by the penitential season of Lent of warning his flock against the dangers of teenage dancing or attendance at Trinity College. Taking a lead in his Lenten pastoral of 1950 from Pope Pius XI, he expressed grave disapproval of the practice of 'permitting young women to compete in cycling and athletics in mixed public sports', and quoting papal regulations to be observed by women athletes, he emphasized that it was 'extremely unbecoming for them to display themselves before the public gaze'.[11*]

Northerners, naturally, looked on things rather differently, and in that very year Ulsterwomen formed the Northern Ireland Women's Amateur Athletic Association; but south of the border, women's athletic competition was obliterated for the next ten

---

* Convent hockey players were instructed to ensure that their skirts reached down to their ankles.

years by a stroke of the archiepiscopal pen.

Maeve Shankey from Kilkenny–a grand-daughter of W. E. Thrift–who was a student from 1946 to 1951, is Trinity's outstanding woman athlete. Having concentrated on hockey while at college, winning a total of fifty-eight international caps, she married and moved north, taking up athletics initially with a view to keeping fit for the hockey season. Her prowess, however, was such that she won Irish titles in every distance from 80 yards to 800 and in the 80 metres, 100 metres and 200 metres hurdles, as well as in the long jump, high jump and pentathlon. She represented Ireland at the Melbourne, Tokyo and Rome Olympics, setting the world's best indoor times for the 440 yards and 400 metres in 1961.

Colin Shillington, an Ulsterman, holder of the college record at 880 yards, was the 1960 Trinity athletics captain. He invited Maeve Kyle (as she now was) to bring a team of women from Ballymena Athletic Club to run in the College Races against opposition to be provided by members of the Ladies' Hockey and Tennis Clubs in the 100 yards and 4 x 100 relay. This innovation, for innovation it was in the Republic of the day, was a success–so much so that the women athletes were presented, at his own request, to President de Valera, who was attending the races. Thus the ice was broken, and organizers of Dublin athletics gingerly included a women's race in their subsequent meetings. But the aura of prohibition did not fade overnight, and it was 1965 before a women's section of Dublin University Harriers and Athletic Club was formally resuscitated.*

Rifle shooting has been a college activity since the middle of the nineteenth century. References exist to a Rifle Club that conducted target shooting along modern lines in the 1840s,[12] while a Board grant to the Rifle Club in 1907[13] was supplemented by Provost Traill's promise (he was a keen shot) to find the money for 'moving figures' and 'disappearing targets'.[14] The club in its present form dates from 1962. A request for affiliation had been turned down earlier in that year on the not entirely unreasonable ground that, given the situation in Ulster, 'it was not a sport which could be conducted in Ireland'.[15] A further application for affiliation was however accepted, provided the club confined its

* A Ladies' Athletic Club had affiliated to DUCAC in 1947.

activities to Bisley;[16] but shortly afterwards the club was permitted to operate in the college once the appropriate safeguards had been established by the authorities. These precautions were taken very seriously; indeed, in 1966 it was reported that the Garda Special Branch was being overzealous in its scrutiny of a member of the club with republican sympathies![17]

The first range, near the Lincoln Gate on the south-east of the campus, was opened in 1965. This was relocated in 1970 on the northern perimeter. With a large membership (currently over three hundred), the club requires immaculate organization, and it has been for many years the premier competitive rifle club in the country.

Trinity won the Leinster Cricket League in 1947 and 1948, after which the rules of the competition were changed to handicap the university club. There was some justification for such a move, as the league was decided on a home-and-away basis, with Trinity playing the other clubs only once; thus if Trinity were successful, the winner would have been decided by mid-June with half the matches still outstanding. It was accordingly decided that DUCC's ceiling would in future be 80 per cent of the points obtainable by the other clubs. The league in this format was won on two further occasions, in 1966 and 1970.

L. Warke, N. C. Mahony, L. C. Jacobson and W. E. Haughton (a big hitter who was also a hockey international) were stalwart run-getters for Trinity and for Ireland, and both Warke and Mahony captained the Irish Eleven. N. B. Hool, slow left arm, and O. O. Coker, a Nigerian who opened the bowling at a brisk pace, then reverting to off-spin, were the outstanding university bowlers after the Second World War.

DUCC won the (knockout) Leinster Cup for three consecutive seasons from 1961 to 1963. The captains, I. S. G. Foster, A. L. G. Rice and G. S. Guthrie, along with most of their team-mates, came from England. With the cup campaign running on well after term had ended into July and August, this posed a problem graphically illustrated by the Leinster cricket career of Jefferson Horsley. A fine squash and tennis player, Horsley was press-ganged into cricket service on the morning of a cup match. His record reads: matches played, one; runs scored, nil; wickets taken, nil; catches held, one; but he won a senior cup medal!

Trinity rugby was probably at its peak in the period spanning the First World War; and although thereafter the Football Club produced many fine teams and some outstanding individuals, there was an ominous gap from 1926 to 1960 in successes in the Leinster Cup. After the Second World War sport in Trinity was dominated by a second generation of South African medical students, and the rugby, cricket and athletic teams resounded with the names of Hofmeyer, de Wet, du Plessis, Mostert and Sang; while on the Irish rugby scene, R. Roe at hooker, J. G. M. W. Murphy and W. R. Tector, full-backs, J. T. Gaston on the wing and H. S. O'Connor on the flank made notable contributions.

For two or three years in this period a flock of peacocks, presented to the college by the staff of the magazine *T.C.D.*, took up residence at the eastern end of the rugby pitch near the Botany School, where a spectacular try might be greeted by a 'raucous chorus of pavonine approval' or, according to circumstance, by a stare 'of that peculiar haughty intensity which the beautiful ones of this world seem privileged to bestow on the unbeautiful'.[18] The peacocks were finally removed after one of the flock had mounted a series of devastating attacks on its mirror image in the highly polished door of a vintage car, the prized possession of one of the senior fellows!

R. D. Hearn, a Trinity threequarter of the 1960s who also boxed for the university, won six caps thereafter in the English midfield. His rugby career ended abruptly and tragically when he broke his neck in a tackle, playing for the Midland Counties versus the 1967 All Blacks. Hearn teaches at Haileybury, where he coaches the rugby fifteen; the courage which he has shown in making light of his handicap, and in living life to the full, has been an inspiration to all those disabled by severe spinal injuries.

Boxing had been practised in the college since the middle of the nineteenth century, but a club was not organized until after the First World War. Robert Crawford, a pioneer railway engineer who entered Trinity in 1847, described himself as 'the Champion in the University' at 'sparring with the boxing gloves.'[19] Mick Leahy, an outstanding Trinity heavyweight, was Irish champion in 1908 and 1909. Returning after the war minus a leg, he won a title as a disabled boxer in 1922. The Australian whom Leahy knocked out in the final had won the semi-final on a disqualification, having been struck on the head by his opponent's artificial arm, which flew off during the contest.

Michael Halliday, captain of the Cricket Club in 1970 and 1971, and Ireland's most capped cricketer. (Courtesy Billy Stickland, a Trinity graduate who was World Sports Photographer of the Year for 1990)

Jonah Barrington, world squash champion, ready to pounce.

John Prior plays decorously forward for Ireland v. West Indies at Rathmines in 1974. The fielder is Gordon Greenidge. (Courtesy Billy Stickland)

The Boat Club defeating Orange Coast College, USA, at Henley in 1981. The crew went on to win the Irish Senior Championships and to represent Ireland in the home internationals. (Courtesy DU Boat Club)

The Boxing Club of 1978 with the Harry Preston Trophy for the British and Irish Universities and Hospitals Championship. From left to right: Michael Telford (featherweight), Mel Christle (heavyweight), Fred Tiedt (club coach: welterweight silver medallist at the Melbourne Olympics), Terry Christle (middleweight) and Joe Christle (light heavyweight). (Courtesy Joseph Christle)

Hugo MacNeill gets his kick away, despite John Rutherford's efforts, for Ireland v. Scotland in 1987. (Courtesy Bill Stickland)

Brendan Mullin racing for the line to score a record-equalling fourteenth international try for Ireland v. Wales at Cardiff in 1991, chased by (from left) David Curtis and Brian Smith (Ireland) and Mark Ring (Wales). (Courtesy The Irish Times*)*

Dublin University Boxing and Gymnastic Club, founded in 1919, has a remarkable record. Since 1925 it has won the blue riband of British and Irish university and hospital boxing – the Harry Preston Trophy – on no fewer than twenty occasions, with ten wins in a row from 1951 to 1960. Outstanding postwar exponents of the noble art include Edwin Solomons (brother of Bethel of rugby and Rotunda Hospital fame); Ivan Millar, Irish welterweight champion in 1930; and R. M. Hilliard, who boxed at bantamweight for Ireland in the Paris Olympics, and, having entered the ministry of the Church of Ireland, was killed as a republican volunteer in the Spanish Civil War. E. F. St. J. ('Toller') Lyburn was a knockout specialist in the heavyweight division who always appeared in the ring wearing a resplendent Irish poplin dressing-gown. Once, for a bet, while on the Holyhead to Euston boat-train, he gave a demonstration of shadow-boxing at every main station on the line attired in his famous dressing-gown. On reaching his destination – the universities championship – he won the heavyweight title with a series of knockouts.

Interest in boxing has waned somewhat in recent years, but a revival was sparked off by the three Christle brothers, Mel, Terry and Joe, in the 1970s. The trio fought, and were rarely defeated, on many occasions for Trinity, and for Ireland; and the names of the Christle brothers on the bill were always sufficient to pack the National Stadium. In 1978 the trio were simultaneously awarded pinks; in 1979 Terry became middleweight champion of France (qualifying by virtue of his mother's nationality); and in 1980 the three brothers established a unique record by winning the Irish middleweight, heavyweight and superheavyweight titles on the same evening.

The professional sporting life has rarely suited the Trinity graduates, or undergraduates, who have attempted it. Jonah Barrington, as good a soccer and tennis player in the 1950s as he was a squash player, is a shining exception to this rule. Committing himself totally to a spartan regime designed to build both skill and stamina after leaving college (where he had compensated in advance by indulging to the full[20]) he won the British Amateur Squash Championship in 1966-67-68 before turning professional, and the Open Championship (in effect, the world title) six times between 1966 and 1972, besides capturing the Australian, South African, Pakistan, and United Arab Republic (Egyptian) titles. He also proved a highly effective publicist for the game as the popularity of squash increased dramatically in the 1960s and 1970s. Other outstanding squash players of this era were Donald Pratt, a nephew of George McVeagh who inherited his uncle's skill at squash, tennis, hockey and cricket, winning the Irish Squash Championship ten times and also captaining Ireland at cricket; and Leland Lyons, a stylish modern historian who played ten times for Ireland from 1949 before becoming a fellow, and finally Provost in 1974.

By 1960 DUCAC had accepted coaching as an integral part of club activity, providing essential background organization together with physical and athletic development for the often somewhat casually organized student clubs. Coaches such as Tom Maguire (athletics), Robin Tamplin and Chris George (boat), Frankie Kerr and Fred Tiedt (boxing), Patrick and Shirley Duffy (fencing), David Mooney (life-saving), John Douglas (hockey), Liam Tuohy (soccer), Noel Mahony, Joe Caprani and Clarissa Pilkington (cricket), and Roly Meates (football) have given wonderful service to the Trinity clubs besides gaining wide recognition within their own particular spheres. They have been responsible for marked improvements in the individual and team skills of the students who have trained with them, and have greatly increased the enjoyment their club members have gained from sport in college.

It was in 1960, too, that the possibility of running a bar in the upper room of the Pavilion in College Park, then used for serving teas after matches, was first mooted.[21] The flow of funds from Trinity sportsmen and women into the tills of Dublin publicans was galling alike to club treasurers and to the treasurer of DUCAC. However, a report from the Boat Club, which had been running a bar in the boathouse at Islandbridge, emphasized the problems that lay ahead.[22] The Board nevertheless acceded to DUCAC's request to apply for a licence for the Pavilion, on condition that no spirits be sold and that hours of opening be restricted to 3.30-6.45 p.m. in term time and 3.30-6.15 p.m. outside term, with an additional half-hour after cricket or athletic matches in College Park.[23]

The constitution of DUCAC had to be rewritten to encompass the requirements of the licensing laws. The most important change was the establishment of a club to operate the licence which all students and Pavilion members could join–the Dublin University Central Athletic Club, inheriting the old initials. The day-to-day business would henceforth be conducted by an Executive Committee consisting of the officers of DUCAC, six Pavilion members, and six representatives of the DUCAC clubs.

These positions are filled at the annual general meeting held early in the Michaelmas term. Customarily the chairman and treasurer of DUCAC are Pavilion members, normally on the college staff, while the secretary of DUCAC and the secretary of the Premises and Grounds Subcommittee are students, with nominations for the six incoming Pavilion members being traditionally put forward by the outgoing committee. In recent years the number of club representatives has been increased from six to eight, preserving an even balance between the student and Pavilion members on the committee. The election of club representatives is always fiercely contested, and is a highlight of the annual meeting in the autumn, which attracts an attendance of some three or four hundred sporting enthusiasts.

The Finance Committee, which formerly met to sift through grant applications and to make recommendations before the meetings of the main committee, was abolished, and replaced by a Standing Committee consisting of the chairman, secretary, and treasurer of DUCAC. This committee deals with grant applications, bringing only those that are not of a routine nature to the attention of the Executive. The Standing Committee also acts as DUCAC watchdog during the vacation. The new constitution, drawn up by chairman John Luce, was accepted at an extraordinary general meeting held on 26 April 1961,[24] and in October the Pavilion Bar was open for business.

Captain Shaw had retired as treasurer at the previous annual meeting, having completed thirty-five years in office, during which time the number of affiliated clubs had doubled. The constitution had proved somewhat hazy about the appointment of his successor, but after some deliberation E. H. Thornton, an Englishman and lecturer in statistics, was appointed to succeed him. As a member of the committee, Thornton had proved a vigorous critic of what he regarded as the antiquated system operated by his predecessor. His own methods were to prove rather too streamlined for DUCAC.

In an effort to provide extra floor space in the Gymnasium,

the Trinity Trust (which raises money from graduates) made a generous grant of £3500 towards the building of a ceiling over the squash courts, which were incorporated in the gym. The Board then offered a matching sum, and this arrangement provided much-needed space for the Table Tennis Club, which was founded in 1951, as well as a permanent home for the boxing ring.[25]

Three years after his appointment as treasurer, Thornton announced that he was spending two terms' leave of absence at the University of Ankara. He never returned to Dublin, and to obtain information concerning DUCAC's financial situation his successor, Simon Newman, was forced to rely on bank statements. The accounts showed assets of £4300 against liabilities of £6000.[26] Repeated requests for an explanation of these figures, and for the return of the missing account books, failed to elicit a response.

In 1963 Winifred Matthews and Shirley Davis, who were already members of the college staff, were appointed to do part-time secretarial work for DUCAC.[27] Winifred Matthews, who was the first woman to serve on the Executive Committee, gave sterling service, particularly to the Pavilion members, over a considerable period, resigning eventually in 1978 from the exalted, if not very taxing position of senior honorary treasurer.

Because of an outbreak of foot-and-mouth disease in cattle in Britain in 1967, the British and Irish governments jointly appealed for a cessation of unnecessary travel between the two countries, which led to cancellation of tours to and from the United Kingdom during the winter of 1967-68. On a more cheerful note, a proposal was accepted for the construction of an all-weather hockey pitch at Santry,[28] and in response to a questionnaire from the Vice-Provost concerning the involvement of the student body in the running of the university, the Executive Committee replied that 'the method by which DUCAC business is conducted is satisfactory and should be extended within College'.[29]

After the Second World War, stand tickets to international rugby matches at Lansdowne Road were distributed to the clubs by the provincial branches on the basis of membership. Students rarely purchased stand tickets, so in the case of university clubs the calculation was based on senior membership. The Football Club had no senior membership scheme of its own, so the calculation, as far as DUFC was concerned, was based on the Pavilion membership of DUCAC. A serious problem arose with the arrival of the South African Springbok touring team in 1969. Anti-apartheid feeling ran high in the college, so DUCAC declined to distribute tickets to Pavilion members for the South African game, as well as intimating to the IRFU that permission would not be granted to the visiting team to hold their customary pre-match training sessions in the College Park.[30] However, this was not enough to satisfy the activists. At an extraordinary general meeting called for December, a proposal to insert a clause into the constitution prohibiting DUCAC from discrimination on the grounds of race, colour, or creed was defeated, after some heated argument, by 69 votes to 27. The activists then sought secession of the Football Club from the IRFU as a mark of disapproval of the Springbok tour. It was pointed out what a disastrous effect this would have on the playing of rugby within the university, and a proposal to discipline the club by withholding its grant was withdrawn in the face of overwhelming opposition.[31]

The first proper soccer match in Ireland, according to the *Irish Sportsman* of 26 October 1878, took place in Belfast between the Scottish clubs Queen's Park and Caledonian. The paper commented scathingly, 'We scarcely think the natives will take kindly to the innovation', and described the unfortunate Scots 'butting at the ball like a pack of goats'. The Irish Football Association was formed in Belfast in 1880. After partition the administration of soccer split, with the IFA in charge of the game in Northern Ireland and the newly-formed Football Association of Ireland playing the same role in the Free State. Many of Trinity's early soccer matches were against regimental teams. The Association Football Club played its first match outside Dublin against a Belfast Selected Eleven in 1884, and in the same season travelled to Bangor in Wales; in Dublin competition the club regularly played second fiddle to Bohemians FC, founded in 1890.

Before the First World War the Trinity club played first in the Leinster Cup and later in the Leinster League and Irish Cup. Between the wars the club had a somewhat haphazard existence, and after the Second World War it suffered by comparison with its powerful rival in UCD. The more recent past has seen a revival in the club's fortunes, stemming from a more professional approach to coaching and training. Robert Prole, a stylish wing-half, and forwards Paul Connellan and Paul MacNaughton (who was also an Irish rugby international), won amateur caps for the Republic of Ireland, while Terry Wickham and Pat Finucane* were particularly talented wingers.

The strength of the university Sailing Club, founded in 1931, derives principally from the high proportion of Trinity students reared on the shores of Dublin Bay. The consequent influx of talent has been materially assisted by the links forged firstly with the Royal Irish Yacht Club and latterly with the Royal St George Yacht Club, both situated in Dún Laoghaire; and over the years the Sailing Club has amassed a series of formidable performances in Irish, British and European university championships. The club's finest hour came in 1980, when David Wilkins and David Wilkinson, two recent graduates, won silver medals sailing a Flying Dutchman at the Moscow Olympics. These notable achievements were rewarded in 1989 when, through the good offices of the Provost, Dr W. A. Watts, a generous subvention made to Trinity by the Annheuser-Busch corporation was passed on to the club and used to purchase a fleet of six fibre-glass Larks.

Spanning the Second World War, Trinity produced two outstanding athletes in the heavyweight division. Leonard Horan won thirteen Irish championships, one for the decathlon, three for the javelin and nine for the shot-put, only to be surpassed by David Guiney, who was Irish shot-put champion on thirteen occasions and won the long jump title once. Guiney, now a distinguished sporting journalist, won the British Amateur Athletic Association shot-put title in 1946 and 1947, while in 1951 R. D. W. Miller became the first Irishman to throw the javelin over 200 feet.

Although the Harriers and Athletic Club has recently produced a string of fine long-distance runners, such as Kingston Mills, Noel Harvey, and Roy Dooney, the outstanding Trinity athlete of the modern era is John Dillon, a medical student from 1968 to 1974. Dillon was practically invincible over any distance from 200 to 800 yards, and as anchorman could be relied upon to make up impossible distances in the relay. One of his finest performances came in the Colours Match against UCD in the College Park in 1971, in which he won the 100, 200 and 440 yards flat races

---

* A solicitor working in his native city of Belfast, Finucane was a victim of civil strife in Ulster, being shot dead in his home in 1989 by the UDA.

and the 120 yards high hurdles, besides anchoring the winning 4 x 100 relay team. As the light faded, the men's match hinged on the final throw of the javelin by Nigerian mathematician Emmanuel Areo, who obliged by putting the weapon virtually through the window of the Mathematics School at the west end of the rugby pitch. The women, having shaken off the effects of their earlier buffeting at the hands of the archiepiscopate, had assembled a powerful squad. With Jane McNicol invincible over long distances (she won five intervarsity cross-country titles in a row), and Patricia Moran winning the sprints, they proved far too strong for UCD. Earlier in the day both the men's and women's tennis teams had proved victorious over the old enemy, giving Trinity four Colours victories to celebrate on the same occasion. Festivities continued far into the night!

By the late 1960s the ban imposed by the Irish hierarchy on Catholic students attending Trinity had broken down, *de facto* if not *de jure*. The formal lifting of the ban was marked by the appointment to Trinity in 1970 of a Catholic chaplain, Father Brendan Heffernan. As a Pavilion member, Father Heffernan served for a number of years on the Executive Committee of DUCAC, and was president of the Football Club in 1979-80. Taking into account the fact that student numbers during the Second World War were artificially depressed, Trinity's enrolment (as the chart on page 94 shows) has grown in a remarkable fashion with the influx from Irish Catholic schools, and has more than trebled between 1950 and 1990. This has been a welcome challenge for the university to face, but it has put great strain on the college's resources.

The grounds at Santry were now subject to such weekend use in term time that the Pavilion had to be extended. In 1969 the Board agreed to finance this extension by means of an interest-free loan of £24,000 to the Capitation Committee and to excuse DUCAC the interest due on the existing loan.[32] The old gymnasium was also proving quite incapable of catering for the upsurge of interest in indoor sports, and the construction of a modern, fully equipped sports hall had become an urgent necessity. The treasurer, Trevor West, was directed to inspect sports halls in British universities.[33]

Trouble was looming, too, on the financial front, with a deficit accruing on the Pavilion Bar and a steady decline in the income from Trinity Week. A substantial meal had to be served during the Trinity Ball to satisfy the licensing requirements. This had led to an increase in the price of tickets, and the ball was losing the support of the student body.

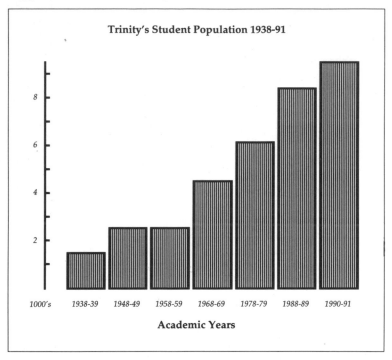

George Dawson, a fellow in genetics and the ubiquitous chairman of the Captains' Committee, was asked in conjunction with the brusquely efficient organizer of the ball, Paul Coulson, to look into the legal problems surrounding the granting of the licence.[34] Having discovered that the ball could be run as an internal affair by making use of the Buttery Bar licence, Coulson assured the DUCAC annual meeting in 1971 that the ball would be 'a different affair next year'.[35]

A major extension to the library had been completed in 1963, and detailed plans were in preparation for the accommodation of arts and humanities faculties on the south-west of the campus, with science and engineering on the Parade Ground at the east end. The Gymnasium would certainly have to be demolished in any major east-end building programme, but the college's city-centre site was constricted, and there was clearly not going to be room for all desirable developments.

It was in this context that a serious breakdown occurred in communication between the college officers and DUCAC. The Board had long since ceased to be the preserve of the seven senior fellows; a greatly-increased Board (student observers attended for the first time in 1971) inevitably led to decision-making being concentrated in the hands of the Provost (Dr A. J. McConnell) and his officers.

A scheme, which had not received Board approval, to construct student residences on the rugby pitch in College Park was put by the Registrar, Dr D. I. D. Howie, and the Agent, Lieut.-Col. J. M. Walsh, representing the college officers, to the chairman of DUCAC (J. V. Luce) and the treasurer (T. T. West) as a *fait accompli*. The *quid pro quo* was to be the inclusion of the first stage of a sports hall in the plan. The scheme was flatly rejected by the DUCAC representatives, and an article in the *Irish Times*[36] giving an outline of what was proposed met with a hostile reaction from students and graduates,[37] from sportsmen and women of all codes, and from Dubliners generally. The Executive Committee of DUCAC and the Captains' Committee combined to reject the proposals out of hand; and in the light of such overwhelming opposition the plan to build on College Park was quietly forgotten.[38] However, even such a dark cloud may have a silver lining; and an unexpected bonus was a Board decision to include two squash courts and a hall (used mainly by the Badminton Club) in an extension of the buildings on the Trinity Hall site.

Mrs Joan Taylor was appointed as the permanent secretary of DUCAC in 1970, and for the first time the office on the top floor of no. 27, Trinity College, was open at regular hours. Paul Coulson's confident assertion in the autumn of 1971 of the profitability of the following Trinity Ball was triumphantly borne out, and at the next annual general meeting he announced a surplus of £1500 compared with a loss of £800 on the previous occasion.[39] A suggestion from the floor that this windfall be used to effect a proper reorganization of the Pavilion Bar was well received, and a subcommittee consisting of Trevor West (treasurer), Aidan Duggan (a Pavilion member from the college administration), and Coulson himself, was established to examine the feasibility of setting up a bar with regular opening hours and adequate facilities.[40] The subcommittee reckoned on a stable profit from the Trinity Ball of £1500 a year for three years, together with a grant from Trinity Trust, whose support for DUCAC over the years had been encouragingly consistent.

There was thus a sum of £5500 to play with; and the subcommittee's proposals, costed at £9000, were promptly accepted by the DUCAC Executive.[41] In spite of the inevitable cost overrun, a superhuman effort made during the following spring and summer, particularly by Coulson (who was sitting his finals), resulted in the opening of a comfortable, properly equipped Pavilion Bar, with a permanent steward, less than twelve months after the meeting at which the proposal had been floated.

The bar proved such a success with its sporting patrons that by 1976 the outlay had been recovered. On returning to Dublin some years after graduation, Paul Coulson was appointed chairman of the Pavilion Bar Subcommittee, the other members being Messrs West and Duggan. Presenting his report to the annual meeting of 1982, Coulson brusquely remarked that while tax and inflation had taken their toll, 'the high level of ranting', particularly in the first term, had proved ample compensation.[42]

The plans for a sports hall had not been lost sight of, and in 1974 the Board approved the appointment of a physical recreation officer to plan and manage the proposed hall and to assist the sports clubs generally.[43] Terry McAuley, a soccer-playing Trinity graduate from Belfast, with experience in Loughborough and Queen's University, took up this post in October 1980.

A compromise was reached between the Higher Education Authority and the college by which a government-funded two-storey sports hall would be built on the campus, with a 9.3 m. high, 20 by 40 sq. m. main hall, six squash courts, a weights room, changing-rooms and viewing galleries. The ground floor was to contain a minor hall 5.4 m. in height, and the compromise centred around the use of this as a science library until a new library could be incorporated in the development of the east end of the college.

A Sports Hall Committee was set up, chaired by W. J. L. Ryan, a fellow and distinguished economist, and advised by Alastair McDonald, who had been largely responsible for the development of the sports hall in Queen's University, Belfast. The architects appointed were Scott, Tallon and Walker. Everything ran smoothly until, at a late stage in the construction, it became clear that the plaster available for the walls of the squash courts would require considerable maintenance. The decision was taken to use panelling to finish the courts, the cost overrun of £21,000, which was DUCAC's responsibility, to be recovered through the imposition of a court booking fee.[44]

The Luce Hall was dedicated on 21 April 1982. John Luce had retired as chairman of DUCAC six years earlier,[45] and the hall was named to mark the contribution he and his father had made to sport in Trinity. A plaque displayed inside the building reads:

THE LUCE HALL

HONOURING

A. A. LUCE AND J. V. LUCE

SENIOR FELLOWS AND SPORTSMEN

Before he retired, Luce had had to fight one further important battle. The Students' Union had made a concerted effort to get control of the capitation fund. The union, the Central Societies' Committee (representing the many college societies), and DUCAC were the main beneficiaries of the fund, and had roughly equal representation on the Capitation Committee. This committee was, like all college committees, subject to the overriding authority of the Board. Nevertheless the Board normally allowed it a great deal of autonomy, and any tilting of the delicate internal balance in favour of one of the beneficiaries would have been seriously detrimental to the other interests.

In 1975 the Students' Union organized a referendum among the student body seeking control of the disbursement of the capitation fund. DUCAC was firmly opposed to such a move, and the Executive Committee combined with the Captains' Committee to issue a circular outlining the difficulties the sports clubs would face should the disbursement of the capitation fund pass under Students' Union control. College societies and the Central Societies' Committee also firmly opposed the change; and after some intensive lobbying during the referendum, members of clubs and societies went in large numbers to the ballot box, and as a result the proposal was roundly defeated.[46]

8

Current Affairs

The opening of the Luce Hall coincided with considerable growth in the student population allied to an increase in the number of clubs affiliated to DUCAC. Aikido and karate as well as canoeing and orienteering were added to a list which already included such 'outward bound' sports as riding, climbing and potholing. A climbing wall at one end of the main hall has proved an excellent training ground for budding mountaineers.

Fencing has been practised in Trinity since the college was founded, as duelling was commonplace among the gentry for one hundred and fifty years thereafter. John Hely-Hutchinson, Provost from 1774 to 1794, promoted fencing as a manly accomplishment, and a Gentlemen's Club of the Sword existed in college in the eighteenth century. The present Fencing Club dates from 1941 and has blossomed in the Luce Hall. For many years one of Ireland's premier fencing clubs, Trinity has produced a string of international and Olympic fencers, and in 1990-91 the club retained the Russell cup for Irish intervarsity fencing for a remarkable thirteenth consecutive year.

Club affiliation was by no means an automatic process: clubs had to exist for at least a year, and had to be well supported and well organized, with constitutions that were in harmony with DUCAC's rules, before the Executive Committee would send forward an affiliation to be ratified at an annual meeting. Three requests for affiliation were turned down at this time: hang gliding[1]* and parachuting,[2] on the basis of safety, and gliding,[3] on the grounds of cost. Virtually the entire membership of the Parachuting Club ended up in hospital after a training week-end in their probationary year, reinforcing the fears expressed before the event by the Executive Committee.

* The embryo club had been optimistically named 'Leonardo'!

The opening of the Luce Hall was to a great extent responsible for the marked growth in female participation in college sport, although the lack of the minor hall (inhabited by the Science Library) meant that accommodation problems lay ahead. In particular the Boxing and Table Tennis Clubs, which had formerly occupied the floor over the old squash courts, now found this space requisitioned for library storage. Table tennis tables and the boxing ring had been permanent fixtures on this floor, and, apart from timetabling problems, there was no chance that immovable equipment could be installed in the main hall.

Trevor West succeeded John Luce as chairman of DUCAC in 1976. With rugby and cricket pedigrees and, like W. E. Thrift, a spell as a university representative in parliament, he had been elected to the Executive Committee shortly after his appointment as lecturer in mathematics in 1966. One year later he succeeded Simon Newman as treasurer, and his nine years' experience of the DUCAC accounts was to stand him in good stead on his elevation to the chairmanship.

One of the first grant applications which he had to assess stood somewhat out of the ordinary. The Football Club, in conjunction with their great rivals UCD, had suspended their entire First Fifteen as a result of ungentlemanly behaviour on the field during the Colours Match at Lansdowne Road in December 1977. The Second Fifteen was then called on to fulfil a long-standing away fixture against the First Fifteen of one of the leading Ulster clubs. The DUCAC practice was to pay travel expenses only for first teams, but as the Football Club on this occasion deemed the Second Fifteen to be its First, the travel expenses were paid, and the Second Fifteen went on to acquit itself well in the circumstances.[4]

The Swimming Club, which had been founded in 1897, was dominated in its early years by members of the Dockrell and Beckett families. The brothers H M and G S Dockrell were Irish champions at the beginning of the century, as were James and George Beckett. Further members of the Dockrell family to add lustre to the university Swimming Club (which led the way in Leinster water-polo for many years) were T. H., K. B. and R. B.; and Marguerite Dockrell (daughter of H. M.) won Irish championships on nine occasions between 1926 and 1933, while N. M. Purcell won a gold medal with the British water-polo team at the 1920 Antwerp Olympics.

In the more recent past Trinity has dominated the Irish intervarsity swimming and water-polo championships, and the standards in the Swimming Club remain extremely high, even though nowadays the top competitive swimmers reach their peak before they enter university. A considerable sum has to be spent annually on pool hire for the club, and also for the Sub-Aqua Club, which affiliated to DUCAC in 1969, but the frightening capital and recurrent costs have inhibited the university from developing its own pool. A solution to this problem remains to be found.

Although the capitation fee was increasing (from £5 in 1957 to £54* in 1990), this was more than offset by the funding requirements of new clubs and greater numbers of participants. In 1977 a decision was taken to extend the Pavilion at the rear, providing extra changing-rooms and more space for the Pavilion Bar.[5] The college agreed to bear the ground-floor costs, with DUCAC paying for the extension of the bar on the first floor. The contract was poorly supervised, and led to a cost over-run. Eventually a deal was hammered out by which DUCAC was granted a low-interest loan, allowing its costs of £70,000 to be paid off over a ten-year period.[6]

Another problem that urgently needed to be tackled was the resurfacing of the hard tennis courts in Botany Bay. The projected cost was over £20,000, and this additional burden would have placed an enormous strain on DUCAC's already thinly stretched resources. The college, however, through its Provost, Dr W. A. Watts, gave generous support of £10,000; and an ingenious fund-raising campaign was carried out via the Knights of the Campanile, whose distinctive tie in dark blue, silver and pink was much in demand among the seven hundred Knights scattered across the globe. A tastefully designed card bearing the colours was sent to all Knights, offering the tie (whose cost price was £5) for £20, the residue after postage and other expenses being directed towards the new tennis courts. The scheme produced the splendid sum of £3000, which, taken with the college grant, meant that DUCAC could fund the balance. One card, from a distinguished Trinity cricketer, arrived with a Paris

* This includes a sum of £10 levied by the Board in 1989 to defray the cost of student services.

postmark, a cheque, and the following inscription: 'Delighted to help the tennis court appeal. Don't bother to send me a tie. I never wear one. Sam.' It came, of course, from Nobel Prize winner, and Knight of the Campanile, Samuel Beckett.

Faced with this upsurge in capital spending, Dr Seán Barrett, lecturer in economics and the new DUCAC treasurer, was forced to exercise exceptional vigilance over current accounts. One of the many items of expenditure that he brought to the scrutiny of the Executive Committee was the annual outlay on the traditional dinners at intervarsity tournaments in which Trinity acted as host. As the number of participants in these tournaments often exceeded a hundred, this resulted in a huge expenditure for the host club. To make matters worse, a practice had evolved among the livelier and more inebriated participants of using items on the menu as weaponry with which to bombard their unfortunate colleagues.

Other problems had arisen in connection with these tournaments, which were now annual events in the majority of disciplines.* The rotation was somewhat haphazard, and a university could be faced with great pressure on facilities, together with an enormous bill for the hosting of an unfairly large number of intervarsities in one particular year. As the tournaments often took place in term time, and could last for four or five days, students were sometimes unable to participate. With these points in mind the chairman contacted the Athletic Union in UCD, whose chairman, Professor Patrick Meenan, made it clear that his committee faced similar problems and would welcome any joint action which could be taken to rein in the costs.[7]

There the matter rested until 1984, when the DUCAC committee took the firm decision that it would not in future fund intervarsity dinners, and that in cases of excessive exuberance it would prohibit its member-clubs from holding such dinners when Trinity was host. As a matter of courtesy the chairman wrote to his opposite numbers in the colleges most affected, outlining this decision and the reasoning behind it.[8]

The reaction made it clear that the equivalent bodies in the

* Damage to the boathouse at Islandbridge during a Sigerson Cup function (the Gaelic football intervarsity competition) in 1990 amounted to £7500. This sum was partially recovered through severe penalties imposed on the participating clubs by the GAA.

other colleges were of a similar frame of mind, which prompted the chairman to host a dinner for his opposite numbers to discuss how such problems might be resolved.[9] The occasion was a success, and so much common ground was uncovered that a further dinner was hosted by Dr Tony O'Neill, honorary treasurer of the Athletic Union of UCD (and the leading administrator in Irish university soccer), and then a third in Queen's University, Belfast. From all this it was plain that there was a strong desire to formalize the *ad hoc* group that had been steering the discussions. After long negotiation and a vigorous debate (hardly surprising, in that numerous attempts at confederation[10] had been made since 1925), a constitution was drawn up for a body to be known as the Council of University Sports Administrators in Ireland (CUSAI), and in 1986 this was accepted by the constituent bodies concerned.[11]

The aim of the council is the promotion and development of university sport in Ireland, 'particularly at intervarsity and international student level', and membership is restricted to institutions participating in a wide range of intervarsity competitions in Ireland. Affiliation to the council takes place through bodies such as DUCAC 'in which student, staff, and professional sports administrators may participate'. The institutions apart from Trinity which initially affiliated to the council were University College, Dublin; University College, Cork; University College, Galway; Queen's University, Belfast; University of Ulster; St Patrick's College, Maynooth; NIHE, Dublin (now Dublin City University); NIHE, Limerick (now Limerick University); and Thomond College, Limerick.

Although international student sport involves Irish students who may be studying in colleges other than those listed, the Fédération Internationale du Sport Universitaire (FISU) recognizes CUSAI as the appropriate Irish body to affiliate to it, thus enabling Irish teams and individuals to participate in world student sports competitions.

A feature of the changing university scene, related to the emergence of CUSAI, is the number of sports in which combined Irish university teams now take the field at representative level. The selection of such combinations clearly requires more than just an *ad hoc* committee, and the appropriate structures need to be established. Rugby was probably the first discipline to produce a combined universities side, in 1933, and the Irish Universities Rugby Union was set up in 1951. Since that date many of Ireland's finest players have had their first taste of senior representative rugby with the Combined Fifteen. This fact, together with strict adherence to the rule that students who do not play for their university clubs are not eligible for the Combined Universities team, enhances the attractions of university rugby and assists the universities in maintaining their clubs' senior status.

The Combined Irish Universities team has many notable victories to its credit. In April 1965 a Combined Past and Present Fifteen carved its own niche in Irish rugby history when it became the first Irish side to defeat a major touring team, overcoming the mighty Springboks, by 12 points to 10, in Thomond Park, Limerick. The Universities forwards on that famous day were greatly outweighted, and only desperate tackling kept the South Africans at bay. The Trinity hooker, Malcolm Argyle, who lost thirteen scrums on his own put-in, became the toast of Limerick, winning a vital strike against the head near his own line. A mighty kick upfield into touch, followed by a quick throw-in, led to the try that helped to make history.

Although the Collingwood Cup for intervarsity soccer was first competed for in 1914, it was 1945 before an Irish Universities team took the field against an amateur international eleven in a match held to celebrate the UCD club's golden jubilee. The formal organization of a Combined Universities Eleven followed in March 1954, and in the first game the Irish Universities side was defeated by seven goals to one at Tolka Park, Dublin, by an English (Universities Athletic Union) team consisting mainly of English league players.

The organization and fielding of combined Irish university soccer teams requires particular sensitivity on the part of the officials, since the players are drawn from two jurisdictions whose controlling bodies, the Irish Football Association and the Football Association of Ireland,* have (in a situation differing markedly from that pertaining in other sports) remained steadfastly and determinedly apart. Thus, for some time, the Irish Universities XI has been the only soccer team[†] to represent the whole country,

---

* The Collingwood Cup competition had to be suspended between 1932 and 1934 because of difficulties between the two associations.

[†] An Irish student team has recently fulfilled a similar role.

a fact that is appreciated by, and adds to the enthusiasm of, the university players.

A particularly powerful eleven in 1976 that convincingly defeated its English, Welsh and Scottish counterparts derived its motive power from a Trinity-UCD centre-back combination of Tommy Drum and Kevin Moran, who in that and the following year won All-Ireland Gaelic football medals with Dublin. Drum went on to captain the championship-winning Dublin Gaelic football team of 1983, and Moran to play professional soccer for Manchester United and Ireland.*

An Irish Universities Cricket Eleven first took the field for a two-day game against a strong Leprechauns side in the College Park in July 1972. Before this it had been the custom for the Trinity president to include players from the other universities in his eleven for the annual Trinity Week match against the university. An Irish Universities Cricket Association was formed in 1974, and pressure was brought to bear on the British Universities Sports Federation (BUSF) to allow an Irish Universities Eleven to compete in its annual tournament, although the southern universities are not members of BUSF. (Prior to this a combined team selected from Queen's University and the New University of Ulster had crossed the water.) Happily the end has justified the means, for the Irish universities have won the championship on two occasions, in 1986 and 1988, and in 1985 the BUSF tournament was successfully staged in Dublin.

Trinity, happily, still continues to produce outstanding sportsmen and women who have represented their university, the combined Irish universities and Ireland with skill and style. In recent years the Cricket Club has produced such notabilities as Michael Halliday, an off-spinner who won ninety-three Irish caps (a long-service record that almost qualifies him for officership of DUCAC); Chris Harte, an obdurate middle-order batsman; and Hugh Milling, an aggressive opening bowler who finished his undergraduate career at the University of Ulster.

But the most enigmatic and, when in full flight, certainly the most entertaining of the modern flock of Trinity cricketers has been John Prior, a tall all-rounder from Belvedere College,

---

* Irish universities Gaelic football and hurling teams played matches from 1950 to 1962 and from 1952 to 1956, respectively, but were at a disadvantage compared to other sports in lacking international opposition.

who employed a bat of maximum weight to hit the ball hard, high and indiscriminately, and often beyond the reach of predatory fielders. Prior, who played thirty-seven times for Ireland, received word of his international selection when laid low with food-poisoning on a Trinity tour in England. So overcome was he with the news that he was unable to speak but, rolling over in his bed, was violently sick!

Prior's indisposition on this occasion in no way inhibited his entry onto the international scene, for his third first-class ball (against Scotland at Clontarf) hit the top of the sight-screen en route to a garden a couple of terraces back from the ground. The following summer, in another Irish game, Prior turned his attention to the Warwickshire attack at Rathmines. He had reached a score of 80 in approximately half of even time, when the English opening bowler Small was recalled to put a stop to such effrontery. Prior celebrated the bowling change by hitting the next five balls for four, reaching his century in 51 minutes (easily an Irish record). His innings of 119 included twenty-one fours and four sixes!

Although there has been a gap in this century between Boat Club triumphs at Henley (from the Thames Cup in 1903 to the Ladies' Plate in 1977), DUBC has had considerable success on Irish waters, establishing a virtual stranglehold on the Senior Eights championship between 1930 and 1950. In recent years numerous Trinity oarsmen (sometimes entire crews) have been chosen to represent Ireland in the Home International championships, and the Boat Club has more than maintained its pre-eminent place in Irish rowing.

The emergence of women's rowing (Trinity now has a flourishing squad of oarswomen) has led to overcrowding on the Liffey. This prompted the metropolitan clubs to band together to build a boathouse on the Poulaphouca Reservoir at Blessington, Co. Wicklow, which is now the venue for the Metropolitan Regatta. In 1988 DUCAC subscribed the bulk of Trinity's share of the capital for this project, and with space in the Blessington boathouse, the men's and women's crews are enabled to conduct their championship preparations on the relatively placid waters of the reservoir.

The Hockey Club has continued to produce a string of fine players, although both the men's and the women's teams are coming under increasing pressure in what *T.C.D.* in 1911 termed 'the insidious Leinster League'. Jonathan Cole, John Watterson, Charlie Latta and Liam Canning from the men's squad, and Jane Coulson (daughter of the redoubtable Denis), Lesley van Hoey Smith, Caroline Watson, Joanne O'Grady and Deirdre Courtney, have, by their exploits on the field for Trinity and for Ireland, helped to ensure that the university maintains its position as a premier nursery for Irish hockey.

The Leinster Rugby Cup returned to Trinity in 1976 under scrum-half John Robbie, who went on to captain Cambridge, scoring seventeen of his side's points in their 1978 defeat of Oxford at Twickenham. Robbie, who is now a sports journalist in South Africa, was an outstanding captain (as well as a fine cricket and soccer player), and under his leadership Trinity won the Dudley Cup, beating all the Irish universities, and defeating Oxford, Cambridge and Sydney Universities* into the bargain.

Besides the Football Club's victory in the Leinster Cup, 1976 was a vintage year for Trinity sport. A celebration was therefore arranged for the teams from the various clubs that had won leagues, cups or intervarsity championships. All available places on Commons (the traditional collegiate dinner) were booked by DUCAC, and the teams, together with their trophies, took their places in the Dining Hall. The evening proved to be so popular that an annual Sporting Commons is now held early in Trinity term, and the number of successful clubs is such that the Dining Hall is normally booked out on two consecutive evenings.

The Football Club in the modern era has produced an unusual crop of fine players who have gained recognition on the international rugby scene. Philip Orr, Hugo MacNeill and Brendan Mullin, as well as Robbie, have played for the Lions. Orr, with fifty-eight appearances for Ireland, is the game's most capped prop forward; MacNeill, an attacking full-back, scored tries against each one of the home countries; while Mullin, a classic threequarter, is Ireland's leading try-scorer, having surpassed George Stephenson's sixty-year-old record of fourteen international tries. All three were members of the successful Irish team that won the Triple Crown and the Five Nations Championship in 1982 and 1985, sharing the championship with France in 1983.

* The foundation dates of the senior university rugby clubs are Dublin 1854, Cambridge 1861, Sydney 1863, and Oxford 1869.

Both MacNeill and Mullin excelled in other codes, MacNeill as centre-forward on a Trinity eleven that won the Collingwood Cup (the intervarsity soccer championship) in 1979, and Mullin as an international hurdler. Other outstanding contemporaries are Billy McCombe, an out-half and probably the finest kicker the club has produced since Lloyd; Michael Fitzpatrick and Des Fitzgerald at prop; and Michael Gibson and Dónal Spring* at number eight.

As the university's enrolment continued to increase, the administrative structure of DUCAC was also expanding. Physical recreation officer Terry McAuley was given responsibilities in other areas of the college, and as a *quid pro quo*, sanction was obtained for the appointment of an assistant physical recreation officer, one-third of whose salary would be paid out of revenue generated by the Luce Hall.[12] Ita Coghlan, a National University graduate with Strawberry Hill experience, was appointed to this post in the autumn of 1986. This added another string to the DUCAC bow, for, with two qualified personnel, it was now possible, with the co-operation of the Schools of Education, Anatomy and Physiology, to offer a physical education option as part of the higher diploma course in education.

At the annual meeting in 1987 George Dawson resigned from chairmanship of the Captains' Committee, having held the post for twenty-three years.[13] A month later the honorary treasurer, Seán Barrett, announced his resignation because of a conflict of interest with his role as Junior Dean. In this position he had had to take disciplinary action against late-night revellers emerging from the Pavilion Bar, which had now become a major source of revenue for DUCAC. He was succeeded in the treasurership by Ita Coghlan.[14]

Elaborate celebrations had been held in 1954 to mark the centenary of the Football Club, including a match with Blackheath FC (the senior English rugby club), and the first floodlit match in Ireland, versus a Dublin fifteen in College Park. 'It is doubtful whether there is a future for rugby after dark', one commentator wrote at the time, 'with wraith-like figures chasing a ball painted to look like a lozenge'.[15] DUCAC support was again forthcoming

* Spring's elder brother Dick, a fine Trinity captain and in 1971-72 the honorary secretary of DUCAC, was capped at full-back before entering politics to become Tánaiste (Deputy Prime Minister).

in 1985 for a dinner given by the Cricket Club to its members from far and wide, to celebrate its 150th anniversary. Shortly afterwards similar celebrations marked the 150th anniversary of the Boat Club, as well as the centenary of the Harriers and Athletic Club.

Considerable thought was given to the question of the contribution DUCAC should make to the university's quatercentenary in 1991-92. Clubs were asked to make arrangements for the hosting of intervarsity competitions in Trinity during the winter seasons of 1991 and 1992 and the summer of 1992. Besides this burst of activity – in the Luce Hall, on the field, and on the river – it was hoped to mark the occasion by the acquisition of new facilities: a swimming-pool and an artificial grass surface being the two favoured contenders. In the end the decision was taken, one to some extent forced on DUCAC, to carry out a complete refurbishment of the Pavilion – very much the nerve centre and the hub of sporting activity in Trinity.

The opportunity arose when it became apparent that if new facilities were provided for the ground staff at the rear of South Leinster Street, women's changing-rooms could be incorporated into the south wing of the Pavilion. The work, which took place during the summers of 1989 and 1990 under the supervision of architect Arthur Gibney, provided not only women's changing-rooms but also increased changing space for men, higher boiler capacity, new showers, and a patio laid out around the front steps to take into account the building's dual use as a sports pavilion and as a club bar. The total cost, of which the college contributed a fifth, worked out at over a quarter of a million pounds.

The Pavilion reaches the peak of its popularity during that brief but idyllic period between the end of summer examinations and the beginning of the great student exodus to foreign parts. Those who have experienced the scene on a fine June evening, with members standing on the wings, occupying the steps, and spilling onto the grass in front of the building, will not easily forget its atmosphere of bonhomie and euphoria.

Just as the academic side of university life must change while striving to preserve its basic values, so too must university sport provide a dignified response to the pressures of an increasingly competitive modern world. New areas of intellectual endeavour are continually opening up, new problems demand to be solved, and new techniques are required to solve them. But the pressure for change must not be allowed to disturb the balance that universities have maintained between the sciences and the humanities, between the stimulus of modernism and the heritage of the classics, between the joy of learning and the reality of life.

Challenges to the sporting status quo are posed by the world-wide coverage of international sport by the media, by the recently developed and rapidly expanding links between the worlds of sport and commerce, and by the increasing tendency to organize competitive sport on a worldwide basis. The media, with television leading the way, have popularized sport to an extent that would have amazed our Victorian forebears. Commercial sponsorship and government intervention have made participation in sport more egalitarian, and have assisted in the provision of proper facilities and of qualified coaching; while competing in world championships must be the aim of many aspiring sportsmen and women.

There is of course another side to this coin. Commercial values quickly penetrate sporting administration and then the playing-field. The old ethos of participation and sportsmanship is soon overtaken by a 'winner take all' mentality. Games are subtly professionalized as more and more time is demanded from leading, supposedly amateur, performers. Opportunities for cross-fertilization between the various disciplines are eliminated as managers and coaches demand absolute adherence to their particular codes.* Systems of promotion and relegation are introduced that raise the levels of competition, but whether they raise overall playing standards remains open to question.

These changes place university clubs in a difficult position. The highly cyclical nature of university sport means that, in a system of promotion and relegation, university clubs remain particularly vulnerable. If demoted they face the bleak possibility that outstanding sportsmen and women in the student body may prefer to play for outside clubs in the top divisions, thereby lessening the university's chances of re-entering the sporting stratosphere. Sadly, too, some administrators, taking a purely

* In 1934 the Football Club, captained by T. J. O'Driscoll, trained by playing hurling during the summer, the highlight being a match against the UCC Hurling Club in College Park during Trinity Week (the players taking the view that intervarsity matches fell outside the ambit of the 'ban').

mechanistic view, pay little heed to the sporting traditions that universities have established, or to the unique opportunities for fostering budding sporting talent offered by university clubs.

In this context the opening of playing membership of the Trinity clubs to graduates (as has successfully been accomplished by universities in Australia and New Zealand), the recognition of sporting talent at matriculation and the establishment of a proper system of sports scholarships have been mooted on a number of occasions, but these nettles remain to be firmly grasped. Trinity's future, in the sporting sense, is intimately bound up with that of the other Irish universities, while the college's links with universities abroad, especially its historic sporting ties with Oxford and Cambridge, remain of the highest importance.

An average age of twenty distinguishes university teams from those of non-university clubs. This poses real problems in a sport such as rugby where physical maturity is an essential, particularly in the first and second rows of the scrum. There are, however, advantages that derive from this age structure. Student teams traditionally make up for their lack of maturity by taking a more adventurous and less inhibited approach to the game; further, the responsibility for the leadership and organization of student clubs falls, to a large extent, on the students themselves. Those young men and women with a talent for captaincy, or administration, are thrust more quickly to the fore, and the experience they gain is a valuable component of their university life. Their responsibility, needless to add, extends to all the teams fielded by a particular club; the mark of an outstanding club captain is not only the quality of the leadership of the first team but the attention that the captain and committee give to the affairs of the junior club.

Besides the engagements of university junior teams with clubs from outside the college, a constant series of internal activities takes place, such as interfaculty tournaments and indoor soccer leagues. Less formal teams also regularly take the field, such as the Stoics, a long-vacation cricket side in the Victorian era for whom Mahaffy and Traill appeared; the Lincoln Ramblers, a rugby side that travelled at weekends to country clubs before Sunday matches were permitted in College Park; and the Dragons, a club formed by an intrepid band in the 1960s that attempted, with some success, to field teams in every one of the major sporting disciplines. These and other less formal activities, which include a staff golfing association and cricket eleven, contribute greatly to the enjoyment which the participants derive from their careers in the college.

Two quite distinct and not always complementary roles have been assigned to the modern university, the transmission and advancement of knowledge being clearly its premier task. Concurrently, the university is required to train young men and women as future leaders in the many and varied aspects of a nation's life. Plato, recognizing this dichotomy, argued for an educational balance between the physical and the philosophical, offering appropriate challenges to both the body and the mind. As more and more control is necessary of our energies and impulses, and as the pattern of existence offers fewer chances of adventure, of exercise, of bodily tension, or of physical excitement, so more emphasis is being placed on sport and physical recreation, with the opportunities which they provide for developing fitness, for forging human relationships, and for balancing tension and relaxation, striving and achievement. Thus sport is, to Huizinga, a pre-eminent element of modern civilization. Not simply confined to the physical development of strength and skill, sport is also the giving of form, the stylizing of the feelings of youth, of strength, of life—a spiritual value of enormous weight.[16]

Trinity's place in Irish history, its splendid ambience and its famous sons and daughters have all contributed to the university's standing in the academic world; while its residential campus, its city-centre location and its island site have assisted in the building of a collegiate spirit and a sense of community. In the development of this community, and in the fostering of this spirit, the sports clubs have played a not inconsiderable part. To most students and graduates the concept of a university is an amorphous one. Their loyalty develops rather to a club, or a society, to an eccentric professor, or to a coterie of friends. The sports clubs play a role in presenting an image of Trinity to the world; their members are indeed the inheritors of a proud tradition.

Appendix 1

Irish Intervarsity Trophies

Rugby
The Dudley Cup, presented in 1904 by the Viceroy, Lord Dudley.

Gaelic Football
The Sigerson Cup, presented in 1911 by Dr George Sigerson, physician and man of letters, professor of botany and later of zoology at the Catholic University and then at UCD.

Hurling
The Fitzgibbon Cup, presented in 1912 by Dr Edwin Fitzgibbon OFM, professor of philosophy at UCC.

Association Football
The Collingwood Cup. The original trophy, which was lost, was presented in 1914 by Bertram J. Collingwood, an Oxford graduate who was professor of physiology at UCD.

Camogie
The Ashbourne Cup, presented in 1915 by Edward Gibson, Lord Ashbourne, a Trinity graduate, sometime Attorney-General, and first president of the Football Club.

Rowing
The Wylie Cup, presented by Mr Justice Wylie, president of the Irish Amateur Rowing Union, in 1922. W. E. Wylie appears in Joyce's *Ulysses* as an undergraduate racing cyclist. A distinguished Trinity man, he was prosecuting counsel at the courts martial of the 1916 leaders, became a judge in 1920, and served on the Irish bench until 1936. He was president of the Royal Dublin Society from 1938 to 1941.

Men's Athletics
The O'Sullivan Cup, presented in 1924. P. J. O'Sullivan was 'All Round Irish Athletic Champion' in 1891.

Men's Tennis

The Iveagh Cup, presented by the Earl of Iveagh in 1937.

Women's Hockey

The Chilean Cup, presented in 1937 on behalf of the Chilean Government by Señor Bernardo Blejer, consul for Chile in the Irish Free State.

Golf

The Roger Greene Cup, presented in 1942 by Roger Greene, a Trinity and Irish international golfer.

Men's Hockey

The Mauritius Cup, presented by a group of Mauritian students who played for UCD in 1951.

Water-Polo

The Beveridge Cup, presented in 1953. Beveridge was a Queen's University graduate and an international water-polo player.

Boxing

The Gilmore Cup, for the Irish Universities' Senior Championships, presented by Bob Gilmore in 1955.

Fencing

The Russell Cup, presented in 1955. Frank Russell was one of the father-figures of modern Irish fencing.

Cricket

The Mellon Trophy, consisting of a small silver cup mounted on a wooden base beside a carved sea-lion balancing a cricket ball on its snout. The trophy was designed, executed, and presented in 1974 by Gordon Mellon, captain of DUCC.

Women's Athletics

The B. R. Martin Trophy, consisting of a claret jug, presented in 1981 by the family of B. R. Martin, a distinguished Trinity athlete who won the trophy at the College Races in 1871.

Women's Rowing

The Bank of Ireland Cup, presented in 1981.

Swimming

The Anchor Shield, presented in 1985 by Joe Duffy, landlord of the Anchor Bar, Portstewart.

Appendix 2

Riot in 1858

The vigour of Dublin student life after the Famine is illustrated in Charles Barrington's spirited account (obtained from his tutor) of a riot that accompanied the state entry of the Lord Lieutenant, Lord Eglinton, into Dublin in 1858, nine years before Barrington entered the college.

The railings in front of the College were much further out into College Green than they are at present and enclosing quite a large space. There the boys were assembled in their caps and gowns as was suitable and respectful for such a great occasion.

The rag consisted only of cheering and of chaffing the crowd and letting off squibs and crackers . . .

The Dean beforehand had deprived them of all walking sticks [and, according to the official account,* 'of a bundle of sticks such as they use in hurling']. A Col. Brown[e] was directing the proceedings, an Englishman and an indifferent horseman. His mount made a buck when a squib exploded near him. The boys cheered and the crowd laughed and shouted. The gallant old soldier was shot on[to] his horse's neck and clung on there unable to get back to his saddle–yells from the crowd. The police came and got hold of his horse and conveyed him back to his seat.

Then he went just wild. An half troop of the Scots Greys were in attendance. Brown[e] took the section of the Riot Act out of his hat. Read it–then ordered the captain of the Greys to, at once 'disperse this riotous crowd.'

The captain of the Greys refused to act, for Browne, a veteran of the Peninsular War, was a police officer. Browne then ordered the foot police to break open the gate leading to the Trinity precincts, and the mounted police to disperse the students. The police had some trouble in breaking the lock on the outside gate.

It was a difficult and long job and all the time they were treated with fireworks by the boys and jeers by the crowd. Meantime the boys got

* R. B. McDowell, 'A Riot at the Gate' (*Trinity*, vol. 9 [1957], pp. 23-5).

ready taking off their gowns and twisting them round their left arms for protection.

At last the gate gave way. In rushed the police with drawn batons and the horse police with drawn sabres after them.

The 'delicate' boys bolted for the wicket into the College but the hardy one[s] stood their ground, presumably the footballers!! They put up a great fight with their fists [while the horse police were] galloping around slashing at the boys with their sabres. The Dean would not allow the big gate to be opened for fear of worse trouble inside the College. Thus the boys could not escape or only very slowly through the wicket . . .

Mr. Mooney my tutor told me all this . . . He was in it. He tried to bolt but could not get through the wicket . . . A horse policeman made a slash at him. Mr. Mooney ducked and the sword went bang into the wood of the gate, whistling by his head. It stuck so hard in the wood the man could not get it out. But the boys got it in a jiffy and made great play of it against the enemy . . . *

* Charles Barrington to E. J. Watson, 18 November 1929, TCD/MUN/CLUB/ RUGBY F./38/11.

Appendix 3

Boat Club Reminiscences

by Major M. P. Leahy

(a member of the crew that won the Thames Cup in 1903)

This account of life in DUBC at the turn of the century is taken from Kenneth C. Bailey, *A History of Trinity College, Dublin, 1892-1945*, pp. 102-3.

It was in 1899 that I joined the D.U. Boat Club, which I captained in 1904. Dear old John Craig Davidson and 'father' Abraham [Stoker] of Botany Bay (who became a famous writer) were the first to initiate me into the joys and sorrows of rowing. The joys were many and the sorrows few: blistered hands and (with apologies) a blistered seat were the only sorrows I have memory of.

Before my time there were two clubs rowing in Trinity (the Boat Club and the Rowing Club). They rowed at Ringsend, mostly in choppy sea water, with planks, dead rats, and flotsam and jetsam of all kinds around them. The boats were frequently filled, and almost as frequently sank, in the choppy seas on which they performed. I think it was in '98 that the two clubs amalgamated and moved to the upper reaches of the Liffey, where they built a delightful Boat House and had a course of one and a quarter miles between Chapelizod weir and the Islandbridge weir, just opposite the Boat House. Our colours were black and white hoops on the rowing vest, and a royal blue shield bearing the arms of Trinity.

In those days we were lucky in our strokes. Arthur Barton, who stroked the successful Tourists' Eight of 1901, was one of the living best. There was only about eight stone of him, but I never met with a better eight stone of man, and I rowed with him all that year. He is now Archbishop of Dublin. Other fine strokes of the day were Haire Forster, and Frank Usher: the general opinion was that Usher was the best stroke at Henley in 1902, and again in 1903 when we won the Thames Cup and lost the 'Ladies' by three feet.

The latter race was rowed at eleven in the morning, and we were completely rowed out when we narrowly lost to Magdalen, the ultimate winners, and the head of the river at Oxford. One of our men, a gallant and powerful oar, was so completely exhausted that he vomited for two hours, and had to be doped with brandy for our final in the 'Thames.'

We were a sad and sorry crew when we were driven up to the start in two one-horsed phaetons for the race against Kingston R.C. at five that afternoon. However, we got going and, after a gruelling race for three-quarters of a mile, Kingston cracked and we won easily enough in the end, though our opponents hung on with great determination and rowed themselves completely to a standstill. When we got to the slip, we were paid a compliment we shall never forget, for the Leander crew, who had won the Grand, were waiting for us, helped us out of our boat, and said that if we cared to join Leander they would be glad to have us. If we cared! There was no greater honour we could desire.

Dear old Andy Jameson sent us a case of champagne, and that night we didn't know much of what happened on earth. I *do* remember Arthur McNeight and I determined to put out all the lights in Henley High Street. He took one side, I the other, and we each had two other men to hoist us up the standards to reach the gas jets: we had nearly completed our mission when the Henley police got into action, but we got the two last lights out, leaving the street in darkness, and then ran. I have painful recollections of scaling a high wall studded with glass, which removed the seat of my trousers and a largish portion of my tail. Arthur, the long-legged devil, escaped unhurt.

The oarsmen of our day owed a lot to the coaches, William Towers, a six-footer, the G. O. M. of rowing in T. C. D. in my day, Andy Jameson, Ernest L. Julian, who was killed at Gallipoli leading his men in attack, Hetty Ryan, Billy Townsend, and Rudy Lehmann, a famous Cambridge coach who came to Ireland, at Jameson's invitation, to coach us before Henley. Townsend figured in a dramatic act put on as an interlude after some Term Races. Billy, who had a most important part, was to be shot. The gun, a huge revolver, was pointed at him and went off with a shattering report, which made Billy completely forget his lines. He stood, trying to remember, then, inspired, clutched his breast, gave a choking gasp, and fell to the ground, muttering, 'My God! My God! I'm poisoned!' The applause was terrific.

I think it was in 1902 that an eight, drifting, rowed out, after a hard race, went over the Islandbridge weir. Before they knew what was happening the stern of the boat hit against the pillar supporting the sluice gates, and the eight snapped in two just between cox and stroke. The cox managed to scramble out, with the agility of which superb coxes are capable, but the rest went over the weir, and so did half-a-dozen sportsmen who followed in pair-oared boats in an effort to help them. Some-one with brains managed to get on to the plank at the sluice gates, cast a rope, and hauled the struggling warriors out one by one. No-one was hurt, and God smiled on us again.

Appendix 4

Rules of American Football
'differing somewhat in rules from that played here'

(from the *Irish Sportsman*, 28 December 1872)

(1) Ground must be at least 360 feet long and 225 feet wide.

(2) Goal must be eight paces.

(3) Each side shall number twenty players.

(4) To win a game five out of nine goals are necessary.

(5) No throwing or running with the ball; if either, it is a foul ball, and it then must be thrown perpendicularly in the air by the side causing the foul.

(6) No holding the ball, or free kicks allowed.

(7) A ball passing beyond the boundary by the side of the goal shall be kicked on from the boundary by the side who has that goal.

(8) A ball passing beyond the limit on the side of the field shall be kicked on horizontally to the boundary by the side which kicked it out, the players not being compelled to stand on their own side, but allowed to hold any position in the field they see fit.

(9) No tripping or holding of players.

(10) The winner of the first toss has the choice of position.

(11) The ball must be started ten paces from the goal, and each side must stand back of the line which is ten paces from their goal. The ball can be babied on the start.

(12) There shall be four judges and two referees.

A rudimentary type of football similar to that described by C. B. Barrington at the start of his undergraduate career in Trinity in 1867 was played at Cornell University in 1871 (*The Dark Blue*, vol. 1 [1871] p. 319).

Appendix 5

D.U. Laws of Hurley, 1879

(from Lawrence's *Handbook of Cricket in Ireland* [1879])

(1) Goals to be *eight* feet in height and *ten* in width.

(2) No hurl to be loaded, or shod with iron, or hooped with wire, in a dangerous manner; the blade of a hurl not to exceed two inches in depth.

(3) Only two players – the half-back and goal-keeper to be allowed to *puck*.

(4) The ball to be hit off from a spot ten yards in front of goal. No opponent to touch the ball till the hurl of the goal-keeper shall have done so.

(5) To obtain a goal the ball must be hit from a position on, or within, a line running across the ground, at a distance of *fifteen* yards from the goal.

(6) A player is on side as long as the ball is on the right side of his person, and he hits it with the left side of his hurl. It is not meant, however, by this rule to prevent a player using both sides of his hurl whilst dodging the ball, although in doing so he renders himself liable to be *shinned*. Swiping with the right side is strictly forbidden.

(7) That a player be hacked by his opponent's stick, should he persistently continue to play with the ball when he has been put "off side" by the dexterity of his opponent [*sic*].

(8) No goal can be obtained in one puck, unless the ball strike an opponent's hurl.

(9) Should the ball be kicked in, or hit behind, it may be brought out ten yards in front of goal and hit off again; but if the ball be kicked by a player into his own goal, it shall count for the other side. If the ball be designedly kicked behind, it shall be considered as still in play.

(10) Should the ball go out of bounds, the first player who shall touch it, either with his hurl or person, shall have the privilege of throwing it out at the place where it intersected the boundary line. If the throw be manifestly partial, the ball shall be returned. The player must not take it himself.

(11) Pushing a man when on side is forbidden.

(12) Should a goal-keeper, although warned, advance more than twenty-five yards in front of goal, an opponent *may* go behind him and still obtain a goal.

(13) A player not to be allowed to wind his hurl round his head when in close quarters.

(14) It is not permitted to crook an enemy's hurl; coming behind "off side" to do so, whilst he is in the act of striking, is particularly discountenanced as dangerous.

(15) Running a ball into touch, unless when the goal is imminently threatened, is discountenanced as opposed to straightforward play.

(16) The ball should always be the object of play.

Appendix 6

Rules of Hurley, 1882

as drawn up by the Irish Hurley Union

(from the *Irish Sportsman*, 21 January 1882)

(1) That the goals be eight feet in height and ten feet in breadth.

(2) No hurl to be shod with iron or hooped with wire in a dangerous manner, nor to exceed two inches in depth of blade.

(3) The ball to be hit off from a spot twelve yards in front of goal. No opponent to touch the ball until the hurl of the goalkeeper shall have done so.

(4) That the goalkeeper alone be allowed to swipe unless the ball be within 12 yards of goal.

(5) That no goal can be obtained unless the ball be hit from a position on or within the twelve yards line.

(6) That no goal can be obtained by a man hitting the ball off-side or with the right side of his hurdle [*sic*].

(7) Should the ball be hit or kicked behind it may be brought out 12 yards in front of goal and hit off again; but if the ball be kicked by a player into his own goal it shall count for the other side. If the ball be designedly played behind it shall be considered as still in play.

(8) Should the ball be knocked into touch it shall be thrown out at right angles to the touch line by a player on the opposite side to the player that last struck it, previously going into touch [*sic*], and when thrown out must touch the ground before coming into play.

(9) A player is not allowed to push, hold or trip an adversary, crook his hurl or throw his own.

(10) A player is on side as long as the ball is on the right side of his person and he hits it with the left side of his hurl. (It is not, however, meant by this to prevent a player using both sides of his hurl while dodging the ball.) Swiping with the right side is strictly forbidden.

(11) If the full back does not pass the half-way flags no player on the opposite side behind him when the ball is hit can play the ball, if it has last been touched by one of his own side, until it be touched by one of his opponents.

(12) A player may be hacked by an opponent's hurl should he persistently continue to play with the ball after he has been placed off side.

(13) A player is not allowed to raise his hurl over his shoulder in close quarters.

(14) No man except the full back be allowed to handle the ball.

(15) That deliberate kicking or throwing the ball be not allowed.

(16) A player be allowed to stop the ball with his feet but not kick it.

(17) That in the event of any infringement of rules 14 and 15 the ball be brought back, on appeal to the umpire, and a bully be formed there.

(18) The ball always to be the object of play.

(19) The decision of the umpire to be final for the time.

References

INTRODUCTION

1 C. M. Usher (ed.), *The Story of Edinburgh University Athletic Club* (Edinburgh 1966).

2 R. O. MacKenna, *Glasgow University Athletic Club: the Story of the First Hundred Years* (Glasgow 1981).

3 R. D. Anderson, 'Sport in the Scottish Universities, 1860-1939' in *International Journal for the History of Sport*, 4 (1987), pp. 177-88.

4 George W. Orton (ed.), *The History of Athletics at the University of Pennsylvania*, vol. 1, 1873-96 (Philadelphia n.d.).

5 T. A. Reed, *The Blue and White: a Record of Fifty Years of Athletic Endeavour at the University of Toronto* (Toronto 1944).

6 Information from the Adelaide University Sports and Physical Recreation Association Inc.

7 *Dublin University Football Club, 1854-1954* (Dublin 1954).

8 *Dublin University Football Club, 1866-1972* (Dublin 1973).

9 M. H. A. Milne, N. P. Perry and M. E. J. Halliday (M. R. Beamish and E. H. Murray, ed.), *A History of the Dublin University Cricket Club* (Dublin 1982).

10 *Dublin University Harriers and Athletic Club: a Centenary History* (Dublin 1985).

11 Raymond Blake, *In Black and White: a History of Rowing at Trinity College, Dublin* (Dublin 1991).

12 *The Old Limerick Journal*, vol. 24 (1988) (Barrington's edition).

13 Letter from Liam T. Mac Cosgar [William T. Cosgrave] to Sir Charles Barrington, 29 July 1925, reprinted in *The Old Limerick Journal*, vol. 24 (1988), p. 122.

1: THE COLLEGE

1 Johan Huizinga, *Homo Ludens: a Study of the Play Element in Culture* (London 1970).

2 Statutes of Trinity College, 1637, chap. 11.

3 J.P. Mahaffy, *An Epoch in Irish History: Trinity College, Dublin, Its Foundation and Early Fortunes, 1591-1660* (London 1903).

4 Particular Book. Provost Bedell's Register (TCD), 11 July 1628.

5 John Dunton, *The Dublin Scuffle: Remarks on my Conversation in Ireland* (London 1699), p. 371.

6 W. Macneile Dixon, *Trinity College Dublin* (London 1902), p. 57.

7 College Register, 13 August 1684; J.W. Stubbs, *The History of the University of Dublin from its Foundation to the End of the Eighteenth Century* (Dublin 1889), pp. 144-5.

8 College Register, 28 July 1694; Stubbs, *loc. cit.*

9 TCD MUN/P/2 74, 82, 94.

10 Map of Trinity College by Bernard Scale (1761).

11 College Register, 3 July 1784.

12 College Register, 7 May 1722; Stubbs, *loc. cit.*

13 Charles Lever, *Charles O'Malley, the Irish Dragoon* (2 vols. Dublin 1841), vol. 2, chapter 105, p. 207.

14 College Register, 23 October 1813.

15 *Ibid.,* 9 February 1850, 11 January 1851, 22 February 1851, 14 February 1852.

16 R.B. McDowell, 'Murder in the Rubrics' in *Trinity* vol. 2 (1950), pp. 20-2.

17 *Dublin Evening Post,* 17 May 1792.

18 Provost Elrington's Board Note-Books, 30 August 1813, 21 May 1814.

19 College Register, 12 October 1831.

20 *Ibid.,* 15 December 1849.

21 *Ibid.,* 6 July 1861, 22 November 1861, 22 March 1862, 17 May 1862, 14 June 1862, 8 February 1868, and 19 March 1870.

22 *Ibid.,* 30 November 1833.

23 *Ibid.,* 19 January 1839.

24 *Ibid.,* 4 July 1868, 13 February 1869, 27 February 1869, 6 March 1869.

25 *Ibid.,* 6 March 1869.

26 *Irish Sportsman,* 8 June 1872.

27 College Register, 19 February 1842.

28 K.C. Bailey, *A History of Trinity College Dublin, 1892-1945* (Dublin 1947), p. 98.

29 *T.C.D.,* vol. 5, 2 December 1899.

30 College Register, 18 November 1899.

31 *Ibid.,* 25 November 1899, 17 November 1900.

32 A. Ivan Rabey, *Hurling at St Columb and in Cornwall: a Study in History and Tradition* (Padstow 1972).

33 F. Marian McNeill, *The Silver Bough,* vol. 4, 'The Local Festivals of Scotland' (Glasgow 1968), pp. 21-3.

34 *Ibid.,* pp. 217-8.

35 Frederick R. Falkiner, 'The Irish Schoolboy Exodus and the Educational Endowments Act' in *Dublin University Review,* vol. 1 (1885), pp. 328-38.

2: THE EARLY CLUBS

1 W.P. Hone, *Cricket in Ireland* (Tralee 1956), chapter 1; Roland Bowen, 'The Iron Duke and Cricket', in *Cricket Quarterly* vol. 6 (1968), pp. 134-5.

2 John Lawrence's *Handbook of Cricket in Ireland,* vol. 14 (1878-79), pp. 11-13.

3 *Ibid.,* vol. 1 (1865-66), p. 11.

4 College Register, 19 February 1842.

5 *T.C.D.,* vol. 1, 12 December 1896.

6 *Irish Times,* 18 June 1880.

7 Richard Holt, *Sport and the British: a Modern History* (Oxford 1989), chapter 2.

8 J. P. Mahaffy, 'Life in Trinity College, Dublin' in *The Dark Blue,* vol. 1 (1871), pp. 490-1.

9 J. P. Mahaffy, 'Old Greek Athletics' in *Macmillan's Magazine,* vol. 36 (1877), p. 63.

10 J. P. Mahaffy, 'Life in Trinity College, Dublin' in *The Dark Blue,* vol. 1 (1871), p. 490.

11 *Aeroplane Monthly,* vol. 5, 5 October 1977.

12 Arthur Samuels, *Early Cricket in Ireland* (Dublin 1888), p. 8.

13 John Lawrence's *Handbook of Cricket in Ireland,* vol. 14 (1878-79), pp. 27-32.

14 *Irish Sportsman,* 3 May 1884.

15 College Register, 7 May 1904.

16 TCD MUN/CLUB/BOAT/1, Minutes of the Pembroke Club, 2 September 1836.

17 *Ibid.,* 20 March 1841.

18 *Ibid.,* 1 April 1844.

19 *Ibid.,* 5 April 1847.

20 TCD MUN/CLUB/BOAT, Miscellaneous papers Box X, 1-29.

21 *T.C.D.*, vol. 3, 13 November 1897.

22 TCD MUN/CLUB/BOAT, Miscellaneous papers Box X, no. 26.

23 Stella Archer and Peter Pearson, *The Royal St George Yacht Club: a History* (Dublin 1988).

24 College Register, 30 April 1881.

25 *Irish Sportsman*, 24 November 1883.

26 *Ibid.*, 10 and 17 May 1884.

27 *T.C.D.*, vol. 4, 14 May 1898.

28 F. P. Magoun, *History of Football from the Beginnings to 1871* (Bochum & Langendreer 1939); Morris Marples, *A History of Football* (London 1954).

29 L. P. Ó Caithnia, *Báirí Cos in Eirinn* (Dublin 1984), p. 20.

30 Archives of the Town of Galway (1527).

31 Mathew Concanen, *A Match at Foot-ball: a Poem* (Dublin 1720).

32 Edmund van Esbeck, *One Hundred Years of Irish Rugby* (Dublin 1974), chapter 2.

33 Asa Briggs, 'Thomas Hughes and the Public Schools' in *Victorian People* (Chicago 1970).

34 W.D. A[rnold], 'Football' in E. M. Goulbourn (ed.), *The Book of Rugby School, its History and Daily Life* (privately printed, Rugby 1856); Marples, loc. cit., p. 114.

35 Thomas Hughes, *Tom Brown at Oxford* (London 1861).

36 *Poems by the late Edward Lysaght Esq.* (Dublin 1811).

37 *Dublin University Football Club, 1854-1954* (Dublin 1954), p. 17.

38 J.E. Davidson (ed.), *Dungannon Football Club Centenary, 1873-1973: a Club History*, p. 9.

39 C. B. Barrington to E. J. Watson, 18 November 1929, TCD MUN/CLUB/RUGBY F./38/11.

40 *Ibid.*, 18 November 1929, MUN/CLUB/RUGBY F./38/11.

41 *Ibid.*, n.d., MUN/CLUB/RUGBY F./38/5.

42 *Ibid.*, n.d., MUN/CLUB/RUGBY F./38/6.

43 *Ibid.*, 23 March 1930, MUN/CLUB/RUGBY F./38/20.

44 Letter from C. B. Barrington, 6 October 1920, MUN/CLUB/RUGBY F./46.

45 C. B. Barrington to E. J. Watson, n.d., MUN/CLUB/RUGBY F./38/6.

46 *Ibid.*, n.d., MUN/CLUB/RUGBY F./38/6.

47 *Ibid.*, 9 February 1930, MUN/CLUB/RUGBY F./38/19.

48 *Ibid.*, n.d., MUN/CLUB/RUGBY F./38/7.

REFERENCES

49 *Ibid.*, n.d., MUN/CLUB/RUGBY F./38/7.

50 *Ibid.*, 18 December 1929, MUN/CLUB/RUGBY F./38/16.

51 *Ibid.*, 18 December 1929, MUN/CLUB/RUGBY F./38/16.

52 T. S. C. Dagg, *Hockey in Ireland* (Tralee 1944), p. 48.

53 Arnold F. Graves to E. J. Watson, n.d., TCD MUN/CLUB/RUGBY F./38/50.

54 *Irish Sportsman*, 16 November 1872.

55 C. B. Barrington to E. J. Watson, 27 December 1930, MUN/CLUB/RUGBY F./38/21.

56 *Ibid.*, 9 February 1930, MUN/CLUB/RUGBY F./38/19.

57 *Ibid.*, 18 December 1929, MUN/CLUB/RUGBY F./38/16.

58 *Ibid.*, 13 November 1929, MUN/CLUB/RUGBY F./38/10.

59 *Irish Sportsman*, 12 December 1874.

60 *Ibid.*, 19 December 1874.

61 *Ibid.*, 2 January 1875.

62 *Ibid.*, 30 January 1875.

63 John G. Cronyn to E. J. Watson, 21 November 1929, MUN/CLUB/RUGBY F./38/31.

64 *Ibid.*, 27 November 1929, MUN/CLUB/RUGBY F./38/31a.

65 Edmund W. Gosse *et al.* (ed.), *The Complete Works of Samuel Rowland* (Edinburgh 1874).

66 Archives of the Town of Galway (1527).

67 Arthur Young, *A Tour in Ireland with General Observations of the Present State of the Kingdom, made in the Years 1776, 1777 and 1778* (Constantia Maxwell ed., Cambridge 1925), p. 202.

68 L. P. Ó Caithnia, *Scéal na hIománá ó Thosach Ama go 1884* (Dublin 1980), p. 436.

69 A. T. Lucas, 'Furze: a survey of its history and uses in Ireland' in *Béaloideas: the Journal of the Folklore of Ireland Society*, vol. 26 (1958), pp. 1-203.

70 Art Ó Maolfabhail, *Camán: Two Thousand Years of Hurling in Ireland* (Dundalk 1973), p. 48.

71 *Irish Sportsman*, 5 November 1881.

72 T. S. C. Dagg, *Hockey in Ireland* (Tralee 1944), p. 3.

73 Edward Marjoribanks, *The Life of Lord Carson*, vol. 1 (London 1932), p. 13; Dagg, *op. cit.*, p. 33.

74 A. P. Graves, *To Return to All That: an Autobiography* (London 1930), p. 132; Sir John Ross, *The Years of my Pilgrimage: Random Reminiscences* (London 1924), p. 22; Dagg, *op. cit.*, p. 35.

75 *Irish Sportsman*, 21 January 1882.

76 *Ibid.*, 27 January 1883.

77 Minute Book of the Dublin University Athletic Club, 1879-85, TCD MUN/CLUB/ATHLETICS/3, 27 April 1883, 22 May 1884, 14 December 1884.

3: THE COLLEGE RACES AND THE ATHLETIC UNION

1 Minute Book of the Dublin University Foot Races Committee, 1866-73, TCD MUN/CLUB/ATHLETICS/2.

2 Programme of College Races, 1883, contained in the Minute Book of the Dublin University Athletic Club 1879-85, TCD MUN/CLUB/ATHLETICS/3.

3 Minute Book of the Dublin University Foot Races Committee, 1866-73, 12 April 1866.

4 *Ibid.*, 4 March 1867.

5 *Ibid.*, 19 March 1870.

6 *Ibid.*, 20 April 1872.

7 *Ibid.*, 15 March 1871 (wrongly dated 1870).

8 *Ibid.*, n.d. 1872.

9 *Ibid.*, 15 March 1872.

10 *Ibid.*, 3 June 1872 and 14 March 1873.

11 *Ibid.*, 6 March and 3 June 1872.

12 *Irish Sportsman*, 26 October 1872.

13 Minute Book of the Dublin University Foot Races Committee, 1866-73, 29 November 1872.

14 *Ibid.*, 22 June 1871 and 24 May 1872.

15 Minute Book of the Irish Champion Athletic Club, 1872-74 (in the possession of the IRFU), 7 March 1873; Gary Redmond (ed.), *Lansdowne Football Club Centenary, 1872-1972: a Club History* (Dublin 1972), chapter 1.

16 Minute Book of the Irish Champion Athletic Club, 1872-74, 22 November 1872.

17 *Irish Sportsman*, 26 February and 30 April 1881.

18 *Irish Sportsman*, 5 July 1873.

19 Minute Book of the Dublin University Foot Races Committee, 1866-73, 31 May 1873.

20 John Lawrence's *Handbook of Cricket in Ireland*, vol. 3 (1867-68), p. 146.

21 Minute Book of the Dublin University Foot Races Committee, 1866-73, 31 May 1873.

22 *Illustrated London News*, 20 June 1874.

23 *Irish Sportsman*, 23 June 1877.

24 College Register, 5 March 1877.

25 *Ibid.*, 10 March 1877.

26 *Irish Times*, 20 June 1878.

27 College Register, 19 June, 22 June, 24 June, 21 and 30 November 1878, and 24 May 1879.

28 Minute Book of the Dublin University Athletic Club, 1879-85, 1 March 1880.

29 College Register, 13 March 1880.

30 Minute Book of the Dublin University Athletic Club, 1879-85, 15 March, 1880.

31 *Irish Times*, 29 April 1880.

32 Minute Book of the Dublin University Athletic Club, 1879-85, 25 May 1880.

33 *Ibid.*, 26 May 1880.

34 *Ibid.*, 16 June 1880.

35 College Register, 5 June 1880.

36 Minute Book of Dublin University Women's Cricket Club, 1946-56.

37 College Register, 3 April 1881.

38 *Ibid.*, 15 February 1908.

39 *Ibid.*, 28 April 1894.

40 W. F. Grew, *The Cycle Industry* (London 1911), p. 53.

41 Oliver St John Gogarty, *Tumbling in the Hay* (London 1939); *It's Not This Time of Year at All* (London 1954).

42 Ulick O'Connor, *Oliver St John Gogarty* (London 1981), pp. 211-15.

43 College Register, 19 May 1877.

44 *Ibid.*, 5 November 1878 and 17 May 1879.

45 *Irish Sportsman*, 3 May 1884.

46 Minute Book of the Dublin University Foot Races Committee, 1866-73, 10 March 1869.

47 Minute Book of the Dublin University Athletic Club, 1879-85, 22 March 1881.

48 *Ibid.*, 29 November 1881.

49 *Ibid.*, 28 February 1882.

50 A copy of the constitution of the Dublin University Athletic Union is contained in the Minute Book of the Dublin University Athletic Club, 1879-85.

51 Minute Book of the Dublin University Athletic Club, 1879-85, 29 November 1881.

52 *Ibid.*, 7 and 15 June and 23 November 1882, 10 January and 24 February 1883, and 3 May 1884.

53 *Ibid.*, 6 March and 23 May 1884.

54 College Register, 1 March 1884.

55 *Ibid.*, 7 July 1884.

56 *Ibid.*, 21 March 1885.

57 *Ibid.*, 1 July 1893.

4: THE GAELIC ATHLETIC ASSOCIATION

1 James Joyce, *Ulysses* (Bodley Head, London 1964), p. 382.

2 John Lawrence's *Handbook of Cricket in Ireland*, vol. 3 (1867-68), p. 150.

3 *Ibid.*, vol. 11 (1875-76), p. 230.

4 *Irish Sportsman*, 1 October 1881.

5 Minute Book of the Dublin University Athletic Club, 1879-85, 22 May and 14 December 1884.

6 *Irish Sportsman*, 17 December 1881.

7 R. F. Foster, *Charles Stewart Parnell: the Man and his Family* (London 1979).

8 *Irish Sportsman*, 24 January 1885.

9 *Freeman's Journal*, 23 January 1885.

10 *Freeman's Journal*, 23 January 1885; *Irish Sportsman*, 31 January and 7 February 1885.

11 *The Irish Cyclist and Athlete*, 1 July 1885.

5: POSTWAR REVIVAL

1 *T.C.D.*, vol. 22, 8 March 1916.

2 *Ibid.*, 28 May 1919.

3 College Register, 1 February 1919; DUCAC minutes, 3 February 1919.

4 DUCAC minutes, 10 February 1919.

5 James Joyce, *Ulysses* (Bodley Head, London 1964), pp. 106, 304, 327.

6 College Register, 1 March 1919.

7 *Ibid.*, 10 March 1919.

8 DUCAC minutes, 30 April 1919.

9 *T.C.D.*, vol. 25, 21 May 1919.

10 DUCAC minutes, 29 May 1919.

11 *Ibid.*, 31 October 1919.

12 *Ibid.*, 13 October 1919.

13 *Ibid.*, 15 December 1919.

14 *Ibid.*, 25 February and 11 March 1920.

15 *Ibid.*, 21 June 1920.

16 *Ibid.*, 23 February 1920.

17 John G. Cronyn to E. J. Watson, 27 November 1929, TCD MUN/ CLUB/RUGBY F./38/17.

18 DUCAC minutes, 8 and 29 October 1920.

19 *Ibid.*, 28 May and 29 October 1920.

20 *Ibid.*, 30 January 1933.

21 *Ibid.*, 11 June 1921.

22 *Ibid.*, 14 November 1921.

23 *Ibid.*, 20 October 1922.

24 *Ibid.*, 12 February 1923.

25 *Irish Times* leading article, 6 December 1935.

26 DUCAC minutes, 16 and 30 June 1924.

27 *Ibid.*, 8 February 1925.

28 *Ibid.*, 9 December 1924.

29 *Ibid.*, 16 March 1925.

30 *Ibid.*, 27 April 1925 and 25 June 1928.

31 *Ibid.*, 26 April 1926.

6: CONSOLIDATION

1 DUCAC minutes, 25 October 1926.

2 *T.C.D.*, vol. 1, 15 June 1895.

3 DUCAC minutes, 25 November 1952.

4 *Ibid.*, 29 November 1926.

5 *Ibid.*, 28 March 1927.

6 *Ibid.*, 30 May 1927.

7 *Ibid.*, 29 October 1928.

8 *Ibid.*, 24 June and 30 September 1929.

9 College Register, 21 October 1905.

10 *Ibid.*, 25 February 1929.

11 *Ibid.*, 26 May 1941.

12 Maurice Bryan, *'DU': the First Fifty Years of the Dublin University Motor Cycle and Light Car Club* (Dublin 1973); Maurice Bryan, *More 'DU': The Sixth Decade of the Dublin University Motor Cycle and Light Car Club* (Dublin 1983).

13 Denis Pringle, *A Short History of the Dublin University Golfing Society, 1909 to 1978* (Dublin 1978).

14 *Belfast Newsletter*, 11 May 1876.

15 *Irish Times,* 15 May 1876.

16 DUCAC minutes, 28 September 1931

17 *Ibid.*, 25 January and 15 February 1937.

18 *Ibid.*, 28 June 1937 and 2 June 1938.

19 *Ibid.*, 15 September 1939 and 30 September 1940.

20 *Ibid.*, 16 March 1936.

21 *Ibid.*, 27 April 1936.

22 *Ibid.*, 3 May 1943.

23 *Ibid.*, 28 June 1943.

24 *Ibid.*, 24 November 1944.

25 *Ibid.*, 20 May 1945.

26 *Ibid.*, 26 May and 24 November 1941.

27 *Ibid.*, 25 November 1947.

28 *Ibid.*, 24 June 1948.

29 *Ibid.*, 27 February 1950.

30 *Ibid.*, 27 October 1952.

31 *Ibid.*, 27 November 1952.

32 *Ibid.*, 30 January and 3 March 1953.

33 *Ibid.*, 2 February 1954.

34 *Ibid.*, 17 June 1952.

35 *Ibid.*, 24 November 1953.

36 *Ibid.*, 4 June 1954.

37 *Ibid.*, 2 March 1954.

38 *Ibid.*, 18 June 1954.

39 *Ibid.*, 1 November 1954.

40 *Ibid.*, 25 October 1955.

41 *Ibid.*, 27 January 1955.

42 *Ibid.*, 27 November 1956.

7: EXPANSION

1 DUCAC minutes, 29 October 1957.

2 *Ibid.*, 2 February 1959.

3 *Ibid.*, 16 June 1959.

4 *Ibid.*, 7 March 1960.

5 *Ibid.*, 27 October 1960.

6 *Ibid.*, 11 May 1959.

7 *Ibid.*, 30 November 1959 and 23 May 1963.

8 Minutes of the Standing Committee of Clubs and Societies (now the Capitation Committee), 17 February 1970.

9 DUCAC minutes, 17 February 1959.

10 *Ibid.*, 10 March 1959.

11 *Catholic Standard*, 3 March 1950.

12 Letter of Thomas Coulter, November 1842, in the possession of Mr Charles Nelson; College Register, 9 March 1867.

13 College Register, 6 February 1907.

14 *Ibid.*, 8 December 1908.

15 DUCAC minutes, 3 May 1962.

16 *Ibid.*, 4 May 1962.

17 *Ibid.*, 10 November 1966.

18 *Trinity*, vol. 6 (1954), p. 13.

19 Robert Crawford, 'Rough Notes of Events in My Life', ms. no. 4 (unpublished), 1894, Dublin University Engineering School Archive.

20 Jonah Barrington with Clive Everton, *The Book of Jonah* (London 1972).

21 DUCAC minutes, 16 May 1960.

22 *Ibid.*, 16 June 1960.

23 *Ibid.*, 27 October 1960.

24 *Ibid.*, 26 April 1961.

25 *Ibid.*, 1 March 1961.

26 *Ibid.*, 6 November 1964.

27 *Ibid.*, 10 October 1963.

28 *Ibid.*, 22 February 1968.

29 *Ibid.*, 11 April 1968.

30 *Ibid.*, 28 November and 8 December 1969.

31 *Ibid.*, 8 December 1969.

32 *Ibid.*, 24 February and 24 October 1969.

33 *Ibid.*, 24 October 1969.

34 *Ibid.*, 5 November 1970.

35 *Ibid.*, 1 November 1971.

36 *Irish Times*, 6 November 1970.

37 DUCAC minutes, 30 October and 5 November 1970.

38 *Ibid.*, 7 December 1970 and 27 January 1971.

39 *Ibid.*, 30 October 1972.

40 *Ibid.*, 8 November 1972.

41 *Ibid.*, 23 January 1973.

42 *Ibid.*, 28 October 1982.

43 *Ibid.*, 21 February 1974.

44 *Ibid.*, 16 October 1980.

45 *Ibid.*, 26 October 1976.

46 *Ibid.*, 17 February and 14 April 1975.

8: CURRENT AFFAIRS

1 DUCAC minutes, 25 November 1975.

2 *Ibid.*, 1 March 1977.

3 *Ibid.*, 16 January 1979.

4 *Ibid.*, 19 January 1978.

5 *Ibid.*, 29 November 1977 and 22 February 1978.

6 *Ibid.*, 17 April and 23 October 1979.

7 *Ibid.*, 13 February 1979.

8 *Ibid.*, 26 April 1984.

9 *Ibid.*, 16 April 1985.

10 *Ibid.*, 8 February 1925, 1 October 1945, 7 March 1960, 16 May 1960, and 2 December 1971; Report of Union of Students in Ireland Sports Meeting held on 23 November 1971 (DUCAC correspondence file).

11 DUCAC minutes, 28 January 1986.

12 *Ibid.*, 28 November 1985.

13 *Ibid.*, 27 October 1987.

14 *Ibid.*, 24 November 1987.

15 *Trinity*, vol. 6 (1954), pp. 10-11.

16 Johan Huizinga, *America: a Dutch Historian's Vision from Afar and Near* (New York 1972), p. 115.

Bibliography

General use has been made of well-known histories of sport in Ireland: Brodie on soccer; Dagg on hockey; van Esbeck on rugby; Gibson on golf; Hall on rowing; Hone on cricket; McElligott on handball; Ó Caithnia and Ó Maolfabhail on hurling; and Ó Caithnia on football. The history of the GAA has been tackled by Puirséal, de Búrca, and Mandle; and, in common with most other historians of sport, the author acknowledges his debt to Magoun's pioneering history of football published in 1938. A number of other works have particular relevance to Dublin University besides those histories of the clubs already mentioned: Kenneth C. Bailey's outstanding survey of Trinity sport in his history of the college covering the period up to 1945; Maurice Bryan's two volumes on Dublin University Motor Cycle and Light Car Club (1973, 1983); Denis Pringle's short history of Dublin University Golfing Society (1978); and Seán Freyne's essay on Gaelic games at Trinity, written to celebrate the GAA's centenary in 1984.

ARTICLES

Anderson, R. D., 'Sport in the Scottish Universities, 1860-1939', in *International Journal for the History of Sport*, vol. 4 (1987), pp. 187-8.

A[rnold], W. D., 'Football' in *The Book of Rugby School, its History and Daily Life*, (E.M. Goulbourn ed.) (privately printed, Rugby, 1856), pp. 147-169.

Blake, Raymond F., 'A short history of rowing at Trinity College, Dublin' in the programme of the Trinity Sesquicentenary Regatta (Dublin, 1986).

Bowen, Roland, 'The Iron Duke and Cricket' in *Cricket Quarterly*, 6 (1968), pp.134-5.

Briggs, Asa, 'Thomas Hughes and the Public Schools' in *Victorian People* (Chicago, 1970).

Cooke, Jim, 'Arnold F. Graves, 1847-1930, Father of Irish Technical Education' in *Education*, vol. 5 (1990), pp. 29-33.

De Búrca, Marcus, 'The curious career of Sub-Inspector Thomas St George McCarthy' in *Tipperary Historical Journal*, no. 1, 1988.

Falkiner, Frederick R., 'The Irish schoolboy exodus and the Educational Endowments Act' in *Dublin University Review*, vol. 1 (1885), pp. 328-38.

Greene, David, 'Michael Cusack and the rise of the GAA' in *The Shaping of Modern Ireland* (Conor Cruise O'Brien ed.) (London, 1960).

Lucas, A. T., 'Furze: a survey of its history and uses in Ireland' in *Béaloideas: the Journal of the Folklore of Ireland Society*, vol. 26 (1958), pp. 1-203.

McDowell, R. B., 'Murder in the Rubrics' in *Trinity*, vol. 2 (1950), pp. 20-2.

—, 'Riot at the Gate' in *Trinity*, vol. 9 (1957), pp. 23-5.

Mahaffy, J. P., 'Life in Trinity College, Dublin' in *The Dark Blue*, vol. 1 (1871), pp. 487-93.

—, 'The Olympic Games at Athens in 1875' in *Macmillan's Magazine*, vol. 32 (1875), pp. 324-7.

—, 'Old Greek Olympics' in *Macmillan's Magazine*, vol. 36 (1877), pp. 61-9.

The Old Limerick Journal (Barrington's edition), no. 24 (1988).

Sugden, Mark, 'A century of rugby football' in *Trinity*, vol. 5 (1953), pp. 22-7.

Strachan, Archie, 'Physical education and recreation in the University of St Andrews' in *The Pleasance Review*, vol. 2 (1986).

Tennyson, Sir Charles, 'They taught the world to play' in *Victorian Studies*, vol. 2 (1958-59), pp. 211-22.

Watson, E. J., 'The Dublin University Football Club' in *The College Pen*, vol. 5, 17 December 1930.

West, Trevor, and Power, Murray, 'A history of the Irish Universities XI' in *Irish Cricket Annual*, vol. 2 (1991), pp. 60-1.

BOOKS

Archer, S., and Pearson, P., *The Royal St George Yacht Club: a History* (Dublin 1988).

Bailey, Kenneth C., *A History of Trinity College Dublin, 1892-1945* (Dublin 1947).

Bamford, T. W., *Thomas Arnold* (London 1960).

Barrington, Jonah, with Everton, Clive, *The Book of Jonah* (London 1972).

—, *Barrington on Squash* (London 1973).

—, with Hopkins, John, *Tackle Squash* (London 1976).

—, with Patmore, Angela, *Murder on the Squash Court: the Only Way to Win* (London 1982).

Blake, Raymond F., *In Black and White: a History of Rowing at Trinity College, Dublin* (Dublin 1991).

Briggs, Asa, *Victorian People: a Reassessment of Persons and Themes, 1851-67* (Chicago 1970).

Brodie, Malcolm, *The History of Irish Soccer* (Glasgow 1968).

—, *One Hundred Years of Irish Football* (Belfast 1980).

Bryan, Maurice, *'DU': the First Years of the Dublin University Motor Cycle and Light Car Club* (Dublin 1973).

—, *More 'DU': the Sixth Decade of the Dublin University Motor Cycle and Light Car Club* (Dublin 1983).

Concanen, Mathew, *A Match at Foot-ball, A Poem* (Dublin 1720).

Crawford, Robert, *Rough Notes of Events in My Life*, ms. no. 4 (unpublished), 1894, Dublin University Engineering School Archive.

Dagg, T. S. C., *Hockey in Ireland* (Tralee 1944).

De Búrca, Marcus, *The GAA: a History* (Dublin 1950).

—, *Michael Cusack and the GAA* (Dublin 1989).

Dixon, W. MacNeile, *Trinity College Dublin* (London 1902).

Dublin University Football Club, 1854-1954 (Dublin 1954).

Dublin University Football Club, 1866-1972: a Pictorial History (Dublin 1973).

Dublin University Harriers and Athletic Club: a Centenary, 1885-1985, A. Gilsenan ed., (Dublin 1985).

Dungannon Football Club Centenary, 1873-1973: a Club History, J. E. Davidson (ed.), (Dungannon 1973).

Dunton, John, *The Dublin Scuffle: Remarks on my Conversation in Ireland* (London 1699).

Foster, R. F., *Charles Stewart Parnell: the Man and his Family* (London 1979).

Freyne, Seán, *Gaelic Games at Trinity, 1884-1984* (Dublin 1984).

Gibson, William H., *Early Irish Golf: the First Courses, Clubs and Pioneers* (Naas 1988).

Gogarty, Oliver St John, *Tumbling in the Hay* (London 1939).

—, *It's Not This Time of Year at All* (London 1954).

Graves, Alfred Perceval, *To Return to All That: an Autobiography* (London 1930).

Grew, W. F., *The Cycle Industry* (London 1911).

Griffin, Padraig, *The Politics of Irish Athletics, 1850-1990* (Ballinamore 1990).

Guiney, David, *Ireland's Olympic Heroes* (Dublin 1964).

—, *The Dunlop Book of the Olympic Games* (Sudbury 1972).

—, *The Olympic Games* (Dublin 1972).

—, *The Days of the Little Green Apples* (Dublin 1973).

—, *The Dunlop Book of the World Cup* (Lavenham 1973).

—, *The Dunlop Book of Golf* (Sudbury 1973).

—, *The Dunlop Book of Rugby Union* (Lavenham 1974).

—, *The New York Irish* (Dublin 1975).

—, *A Little Wine and a Few Friends* (Dublin 1976).

—, *The Book of Gaelic Football* (Dublin 1976).

—, *A Few Days in My Time* (Dublin 1977).

—, *Argentina '78* (Dublin 1978).

—, *The History of the World Cup, 1930-1982* (Dublin 1982).

—, *The Friendly Olympics* (Dublin 1982).

—, *The Carlsberg Book of Irish Rugby* (Dublin 1983).

—, *Good Days and Good Friends* (Dublin 1985).

—, *Ireland v. New Zealand: 100 Years of Rugby* (Dublin 1989).

—, *The World Cup, 1930-1990* (Dublin 1990).

—, *West Germany's World Cup* (Dublin 1990).

—, *100 Years of Golf at Sutton: a History of the Sutton Golf Club* (Dublin 1990).

—, and Purcell, Patrick, *The Guinness Book of Hurling Records* (Dublin 1965).

Hall, T. F., *History of Boat-Racing in Ireland* (Dublin 1937).

Hearn, Danny, with Reyburn, Ross, *Crash Tackle* (London 1972).

Holt, Richard, *Sport and the British: a Modern History* (Oxford 1989).

Hone, W.P., *Cricket in Ireland* (Tralee 1956).

Hughes, Thomas, *Tom Brown's Schooldays, by an Old Boy* (London 1857).

—, *Tom Brown at Oxford* (London 1861).

Huizinga, Johan, *Homo Ludens: a Study of the Play Element in Culture* (London 1970).

—, *America: a Dutch Historian's Vision from Afar and Near* (New York 1972).

Joubert, Arrie (ed.), *The History of Intervarsity Sport in South Africa: Looking Back with Pete Suzman* (Stellenbosch 1985).

Joyce, James, *Ulysses* (Bodley Head, London 1964).

Lansdowne Football Club Centenary, 1872-1972, a Club History, Gary Redmond (ed.), (Dublin 1972).

Lecky, W.E.H., *The Map of Life, Conduct and Character* (London 1913).

Lee, Joseph, *The Modernisation of Irish Society, 1848-1918* (Dublin 1989).

Lyons, F.S.L., *Ireland since the Famine* (London 1971).

McDowell, R.B. (ed.), *Social Life in Ireland, 1800-1845* (Cork 1957).

— and Webb, D. A., *Trinity College Dublin, 1592-1952: an Academic History* (Cambridge 1982).

McElligott, Tom, *The Story of Handball: The Game, the Players, the History* (Dublin 1984).

MacKenna, R.O., *Glasgow University Athletic Club: the Story of the First Hundred Years* (Glasgow 1981).

McNeill, F. Marian, *The Silver Bough* (Glasgow 1968).

Magoun, Francis Peabody, *History of Football from the Beginnings to 1871* (Koelner Anglistiche Arbeiten Bd. 31; Bochum-Langendreer 1939).

Mahaffy, J.P., *An Epoch in Irish History: Trinity College, Dublin, Its Foundation and Early Fortunes, 1591-1660* (London 1903).

Mandle, W.F., *The Gaelic Athletic Association and Irish Nationalist Politics, 1884-1924* (London 1987).

Marjoribanks, Edward, *The Life of Lord Carson* (London 1932).

Marples, Morris, *A History of Football* (London 1954).

Maxwell, Constantia, *Dublin under the Georges, 1714-1830* (London 1936).

—, *Country and Town in Ireland under the Georges* (London 1940).

Mecredy, R.J., *Cyclist and Pedestrian Guide to the Neighbourhood of Dublin* (Dublin and London 1891).

—, *Mecredy's Road Book of Ireland* (Dublin 1892).

—, *The Motor Book* (London and New York 1907).

—, *The Encyclopaedia of Motoring* (Dublin and London 1910).

— and Wilson, A.J., *The Art and Pastime of Cycling* (Dublin and London 1890).

Milne, M. H. A., Perry, N. P., and Halliday, Michael, (Beamish, M. R., and Murray, E. H., eds.) *A History of the Dublin University Cricket Club* (Dublin 1982).

Ó Broin, Leon, *W. E. Wylie and the Irish Revolution, 1916-1921* (Dublin 1989).

Ó Caithnia, Liam P., *Scéal na hIomána* (Dublin 1980).

—, *Mícheál Cíosóig* (Dublin 1982).

—, *Báirí Cos in Éirinn* (Dublin 1984).

O'Connor, Ulick *Oliver St John Gogarty: a Poet and his Times* (London 1964).

—, *The Fitzwilliam Story, 1877-1977* (Dublin 1977).

Ó Maolfabhail, Art, *Camán: Two Thousand Years of Hurling in Ireland* (Dundalk 1975).

Orton, George W. (ed.), *The History of Athletics at the University of Pennsylvania*, vol. 1, 1873-96 (Philadelphia, n.d.).

Pringle, Denis, *A Short History of the Dublin University Golfing Society, 1909 to 1978* (Dublin 1978).

Puirséal, Pádraig, *The GAA in its Time* (Dublin 1984).

Rabey, A. Ivan, *Hurling at St Columb and in Cornwall, a Study in History and Tradition* (Padstow 1972).

Reed, T.A., *The Blue and White: A Record of Fifty Years of Athletic Endeavour at the University of Toronto* (Toronto 1944).

Robbie, John, *The Game of My Life* (London 1989).

Ross, Sir John, *The Years of My Pilgrimage, Random Reminiscences* (London 1924).

Rowland, Samuel, *The Complete Works*, ed. E. W. Gosse *et al.* (Edinburgh 1874).

Samuels, Arthur, *Early Cricket in Ireland* (a paper read before the Kingstown Literary and Debating Society, Dublin 1888).

Solomons, Bethel, *One Doctor in his Time* (London 1956).

Stanford, W. B., and McDowell, R. B., *Mahaffy: a Biography of an Anglo-Irishman* (London 1971).

Stubbs, J.W., *The History of the University of Dublin from 1591 to 1800* (Dublin 1889).

Usher, C.M. (ed.), *The Story of Edinburgh University Athletic Club* (Edinburgh 1966).

van Esbeck, Edmund, *One Hundred Years of Irish Rugby: the Official History of the Irish Rugby Union* (Dublin 1974).

—, *The Story of Irish Rugby* (London 1986).

Wanderers Football Club, 1869-70 to 1969-70 (Dublin 1969).

Winch, Jonty, *An Illustrated History of Sport at the University of the Witwatersrand, Johannesburg* (Johannesburg 1990).

Young, Arthur, *A Tour in Ireland with General Observations of the Present State of the Kingdom, made in the Years 1776, 1777 and 1778*, Constantia Maxwell, ed. (Cambridge 1925).

Young, G.M., *Victorian England: Portrait of an Age* (London 1936).

Index

Dublin University clubs are listed in small capitals.

Aberdeen University Athletic Association, 2
Academy Hurling Club, 55
Act of Union, 8, 11 *et seq.*
Adelaide University Sports Association, 2
AIKIDO CLUB, 98
All England Lawn Tennis Club, 48f.
Amateur Athletic Association, 54
Amateur Athletic Club, London, 55f.
Amateur Athletic Union of Eire, 75 *et seq.*
amateur, definition of, 21, 54 *et seq.*
American football, rules of, 119
Annheuser-Busch corporation, 92
archery, 8
Areo, Emmanuel, 93
Argyle, Malcolm, 103
Armstrong, W.W., 43
Arnold, Thomas, 23
Association football, 23, 91
ASSOCIATION FOOTBALL CLUB,
    55, 91 *et seq.*
Athletic Association of the University of
    Pennsylvania, 2
ATHLETIC CLUB (1872)
    federal body, 2
    income of and grants by, 2, 50 *et seq.*
    predecessor of DUCAC, 1
ATHLETIC CLUB (1885)
    merger with HARRIERS CLUB, 46f.
    origins, 37f.
    prominent members, 46
ATHLETIC COMMITTEE (1857), *see*
    FOOTBALL CLUB FOOT RACES
    COMMITTEE
athletics
    and College Races, 37 *et sqq.*
    and the 'ban', 74 *et seq.*, 76f.
    early use of College Park for, 10
    influence of Sabbatarianism on, 54
    traditional Irish sport, 8
    women's, restricted in Ireland, 73, 83 *et seq.*
ATHLETIC UNION (1902)
    and university colour, 67
    decline of, 60f.
    federal body, 2
    income of and grants by, 2, 50
    minute-book of (1879-82), 2
    predecessor of DUCAC, 1
    rules of, 50

BADMINTON CLUB, 95
Bamford, J.L., 77

Barrett, Seán, FTCD, 101, 107
Barrington, Charles Burton
    account of 1858 riot by, 115
    as oarsman, 30, 43
    biography, 4
    correspondence of, quoted, 25 *et sqq.*
Barrington, Croker, 30, 43
Barrington, Jonah, 87 *et seq.*
Barton, Arthur, 117
Beckett, George, 99
Beckett, James, 99
Beckett, Samuel, 100 *et seq.*
Belfast (later, Royal Belfast) Golf Club, 49
Belvedere College, 104
Bennett, E.H., 30
Bernard, J.H., Provost, 62
BICYCLE CLUB, 46 *et seq.*
Blackheath Football Club, 26, 35, 107
Blankers-Koen, Fanny, 83
Bloom, Leopold, 60
BOAT CLUB
    150th anniversary of, 108
    Blessington project, 105
    history published, 2
    Islandbridge
        bar at, 88
        damage to boathouse at, 101f.
        move to, 21
    merger with ROWING CLUB, 21
    origin of name, 19
    reminiscences of (1899-1904), 117
    successes, 42 *et seq.*, 105
Bohemians Football Club, 47
botanic gardens, Lansdowne Road, 81
bowling green, in college, 6, 7
Bowling Green, Dublin, 6
boxing, 8
BOXING AND GYMNASTIC CLUB,
    86 *et seq.*, 90, 99
Boyd, H.A., 77
Boyd Quaih, 77
Briscoe, A.W., 77
British Universities Sports Federation, 104
Browning, F.H., 43, 45, 59f.
Bulger, D.D., 46, 75f.
Bury, J.B., FTCD, 12

Callanan, Fionbarr, 76
Cambridge University
    1885 bicycle race with, 47
    athletic season of 1895, 3

first boat race with Oxford, 2
first cricket match with Oxford, 2
rugby fixtures with, 44
Canning, Liam, 106
CANOE CLUB, 98
capitation fee
    adjustment of, 82
    committee administering, 81
    control of fund, 97
    increases in, offset by new clubs, 100
    schemes for, 59, 62 et seq., 78 et seq., 80 et seq.
Caprani, Joe, 88
Captains' Committee, of DUCAC
    and capitation fund, 97
    and plan to build on College Park, 95
    and pinks for women, 73
    in abeyance, 71
    origins, 68
Carson, Edward, 35f., 63f.
Carson, Joseph, FTCD, 51 et seq.
Cassels, Richard, architect, 6
Central Societies' Committee, 97
Charles O'Malley, 7
Charterhouse School, 23
Cheltenham College, 23 et seq.
Christle brothers, 87
Churchill, Lord Randolph, 41f.
Churchill, Winston, 41f.
Civil Service Academy, 53
Civil Service Athletic Club, 39
Clifford, R.F.M., 48
CLIMBING CLUB, 98
Clinch family, 65
Coghlan, Ita, 107
Coker, O.O., 85
Cole, Jonathan, 106
College Historical Society, 65
College Park
    affected by hurricane, 10
    crocuses on pitch, 11
    history, 5, 7, 10
    'ha-ha' in, 7
    in First World War, 59
    quality of rugby pitch in, 11
    representative cricket in, 43
    rubbish dump in, 10
    running path in, 39
    sheep in, 59
    'swamp'as part of, 10
    'Wilderness' in, 10
        intervention of providence in, 10
College Pen, The, 3
College Races
    decline after 1880, 46, 60f.
    development, 38 et sqq., 49 et seq.
    origins, 37
    part of Trinity Week, 63
Collingwood Cup, 103 and f., 107
Combined Universities XV, 74, 103

Combined Universities teams, 102 et seq.
Commercial Rowing Club, 20
Connellan, Paul, 92
Conroy, Judge J.C., 76
Cork County Cricket Club, 62
Corley, H.H., 44
Cotter, A., 43
Coulson, Denis, 68 and f.
Coulson, Jane, 106
Coulson, Paul, 94 et sqq.
Council of University Sports Admin-
    istrators in Ireland, 102
Courtney, A.C., 46
Courtney, Deirdre, 106
Craig, J.K., 68
Crawford, Benny, 69
Crawford, Robert, 86
cricket and see CRICKET CLUB
    bat, and modern hurling stick, 11
    first recorded game in Ireland, 13
    'garrison game', 13
    players in College Park fired at, 1921, 63
    postures adopted in, 'indecent', 12
    representative matches, in College Park, 43
    wicket, early, 11
CRICKET CLUB
    150th anniversary of, 108
    after Second World War, 85
    foundation of, 13
    pitch, 10, 13, 78
    sesquicentenary history of, 2
Croke, Archbishop, 56
Cronyn, A.P., 3, 32
Cronyn, J.G., 3, 32, 63
CROQUET CLUB, 48f.
Cusack, Michael, 36, 53 et sqq.
Cussen, Denis, 65

Davin, Maurice, 56
Davis, Shirley, 90
Davitt, Michael, 56
Dawson, George, FTCD, 76, 94 ,107
de Valera, Eamon, 84
de Wet, N.J.B., 86
Dillon, John, 92
Dingle Club, Liverpool, 31
Dockrell family, 99
Dolphin Rowing Club, 20
Dooney, Roy, 92
Douglas, John, 88
Dragons Club, 110
Drew, Sir Thomas, architect, 51
Drum, Tommy, 104
Dublin City University, 102
Dublin Hurling Club, 55
Dublin University and see Trinity College
    history, 5
    proposed merger of, with UCD, 80f.
    Quatercentenary 1991-92, 1

INDEX

D.U. CENTRAL ATHLETIC CLUB
(DUCAC 1960 –)
  and international rugby tickets, 90
  and qualifications of athletes, 110
  and sports scholarships, 110
  affiliation of clubs to, 98
  antecedent bodies, 1
  chairmen, 1
  change from former title, 88
  constitution, 1
  discrimination, motion against, 91
  executive committee of, 89, 95, 97
  finance of developments by, 93, 100
  origin, 1
  quatercentenary celebrations, 108
  records, 1
  standing committee of, 89
D.U. CENTRAL ATHLETIC COMMITTEE
(DUCAC 1919-60)
  accommodation, 81
  birth of, 59
  constitution of, 59 et seq.
    amendment of, 88
  early activities, 62
  financial problems of 1924, 64
  financial system, 60, 62, 67, 78, 81 et seq.
Dudley Cup, for intervarsity rugby, 44
duelling, formerly commonplace, 98
Duffy, Patrick and Shirley, 88
Duffy, Joe, 114
Duggan, Aidan, 95 et seq.
Dunlop, H.W.D., 39
Dunlop pneumatic tyre, 47
du Plessis, K., 86
Dutting, army officer, 30

Easter Rising (1916), 59 and f., 61
Edinburgh University
  Athletic Club, 2
  cross-country contests against, 46
  rugby fixtures with, 44
Ellis, William Webb, 22 and f.
Elrington, Provost, 8
Eton College, 23 et seq.
Exeter College, Oxford, 37

Famine, 12
Fédération Internationale du Sport Universitaire, 102
fencing, 7
FENCING CLUB, 98
Finucane, Pat, 92 and f.
First World War
  effect of, in college, 59
  Trinity volunteers for, 59
Fitzgerald, Albert, 77 et seq.
Fitzgerald, Des, 107
Fitzgerald, George Francis, FTCD
  and the Pavilion, 51
  attempt of, to fly, 16

  role of, in Trinity sport, 14, 16
  Trinity mathematician, 12
Fitzgibbon, E., 113
Fitzpatrick, Michael, 107
Fitzwilliam Lawn Tennis Club, 48
fives, 6, 7, 13f.
foot-and-mouth, outbreak of, 90
football and see FOOTBALL CLUB
  American, 23f.
  Australian Rules, 23f.
  formerly illegal, 22
  parish game, 11
  traditional sport, 8, 22
  violence in, 22
Football Association of Ireland, 91, 103
FOOTBALL CLUB
  after Second World War, 86
  and early international fixtures, 31 et seq.
  and formation of IRFU, 31 et seq.
  centenary celebrations in 1954, 107
  centenary history of, 2
  colours matches, 74
  combined matches, 74
  dress, origins of, 28 et seq.
  early history of, 25
  early university matches, 44
  E.J. McC. Watson's papers concerning, 3
  first floodlit match in Ireland (1954), 106
  foundation of, 24
  in inter-war period, 65
  members of, who captained Ireland, 44
  members of, international players, 32, 106
  novel training system of 1934, 109
  pitch, 10, 11, 43, 86
  rules, 26 et sqq., 29 et seq.
  secession of, from IRFU, proposed, 91
  South African members, 64 et seq., 86
  stand proposed, 70 et seq.
  suspension of First XV, 99
  unorthodox team formation, 67
FOOTBALL CLUB FOOT RACES
COMMITTEE
  and College Races, 37 et sqq.
  DUCAC's earliest predecessor, 1
  federal body, 2
  income of and grants by, 2, 49
  minute book of (1866 73), 2
Ford, E., FTCD, 8
Foster, I.S.G., 85
Francis, Bob, 76
Franks, J.G., 44
French College, Blackrock, 53
Fry, C.B., 17

Gaelic Athletic Association, 53 et sqq., 101f.
GAELIC FOOTBALL CLUB, 78
Galbraith, J.A., FTCD, 52
Galbraith, R., 44
Garbally, Co. Galway, 13

Gentlemen's Club of the Sword, 98
gentry, Irish, notorious for gaming etc., 8
George, Chris, 88
Gibney, Arthur, architect, 108
Gibson, Edward, 42, 113
Gibson, Michael, 107
Gilmore, Bob, 114
Glasgow University Athletic Club, 2
Glenstal, Co. Limerick, 4
Godfrey, F. La Touche, FTCD, 81
Gogarty, Oliver St John, 47
Goldsmith, Oliver, 8
GOLF CLUB
    colours match, 69
    finances of, scrutinized, 72, 77
    graduates' match with UCD, 69
    low estimate of DUCAC's perspicacity, 77
    origins, 49
    Taylor bequest to, 76 et seq.
GOLFING SOCIETY, 69
golf, in Ireland, 49
Goulding, W.J., 32
Grace, E.M., 17
Grace, G.F., 15
Grace, W.G., 17, 43
Grant, Tom, DUBC coach, 20
Graves, Alfred Perceval, 4, 25, 35f.
Graves, Arnold Felix, 4, 25, 29 et seq.
Graves, Charles (sen.), FTCD, 25
Graves, Charles (jun.), 25
Greene, Roger, 114
Gregory, Lady A., 53
Guiney, David, 92
gunnery, 8
Guthrie, G.S., 85
Guy's Hospital Football Club, 25
Gwynn, A.P., 45
Gwynn, E.J., Provost, 16
Gwynn, family of, 16 et seq.
Gwynn, L.H., FTCD, 45
Gwynn, R.M., FTCD
    footballer, 44
    founder member of DUCAC, 59 et seq.
    quoted, 10
Gymnasium
    commandeered, 59
    construction of, 9
    exhibition in, 9
    extended, 89 et seq.
    finance of, 38
    inadequacy of, 92 et seq.

'hacking', 27 et seq., 29
'Hallelujah', 28
Halliday, Michael, 104
Hall of Honour, 70
Hamilton, Horace, 17
Hamilton, Sir William Rowan, 12
Hanahoe, Tony, 78

handball, 8, 9
hangman, assisting, 52
HARRIERS AND ATHLETIC CLUB
    and AAUE, 75
    centenary celebrations, 108
    centenary history of, 2
    formed by merger, 46f.
    match of 1961 with UCD, 76
    'unofficial' match of 1953 with UCD, 76f.
    women's section, 84
Harte, Chris, 104
Hartford, Canon R.R., 73f.
Harvey, Noel, 92
Harvey, T.A., 43
Haughton, Samuel, FTCD, 30 et seq., 52
Haughton, W.E., 82, 85
Hawks Club, 71
Hearn, R.D., 86
Heffernan, Father Brendan, 93
Heffernan, Kevin, 78
Hely-Hutchinson, Provost John, 7, 98
Hereans, 72f.
Higher Education Authority, 96
High School, 35
Hilliard, R.M., 87
Hockey Association, 35
HOCKEY CLUB
    after Second World War, 82, 105 et seq.
    application for pitch, 10
    founded, 47 et seq.
    golden era of, in 1930s, 68
hockey
    relation to hurley, 35
Hofmeyer, J.J. van R., 86
Hogan, Sarsfield, 74
Hone, family of, 16
Hool, N.B., 85
Hopkirk, Paddy, 69
Horan, Leonard, 92
Horsley, Gilda, 73f.
Horsley, Jefferson, 85
Howie, D.I.D., FTCD, 95
Huet, Miss, 73
Huizinga, Johan, 5, 111
hurley, and see hurling, HURLEY CLUB
    distinct forms of, 11, 38
    laws of 1882, 122
    origins, 32 et seq.
    parish game, 11
    traditional sport, 8
HURLEY CLUB
    colours of, 68
    decline of, 36, 50
    Edward Carson a player, 63f.
    laws of, 34 et sqq., 36, 120
    origins, 33
    pitch, original, 10
hurling, and see hurley, HURLING CLUB
    revival of, by Cusack, 55

HURLING CLUB
  resuscitation, 70 and f.
Hyde, Douglas, 53

Ingram, John Kells, FTCD, 21
International Amateur Athletic Federation, 75
International Olympic Committee, 75f.
intervarsity tournaments, expense of, 101
Irish Amateur Athletic Association, 56
Irish Champion Athletic Club, 39, 53, 70
Irish Cricket Union, 18
Irish Cycling Association, 46
Irish Football Association, 91, 103
Irish Georgian Society (1908), 14
Irish Hockey Union, 47
Irish Hurley Union
  laws of 1882, 122
  origins, 35
Irish Lacrosse Union, 70
Irish Rugby Football Union
  origins, 31 et seq.
  Corps, 59f.
  headquarters, 39f.
  Trinity presidents of, 32
Irish Senior Cup (hockey), 68 and f.
Irish Sportsman, 20, 23f., 40,
  50f., 55, 91, 119, 122
Irish Universities Cricket Association, 104
Irish Universities Rugby Union, 74, 103
Iveagh, Earl of, 114

Jacobson, L.C., 85
Jameson, J.F., 77
Jellett, J.H., FTCD, 51
Johnson, C.L., 17
Johnston, M., 44
Joly, John, FTCD, 69
Joyce, James, 54, 60, 113
Julian, Ernest L., 118

KARATE CLUB, 98
Keane, F.B.V., 72
Kelly, J.J., 43
Kennelly, Brendan, FTCD, 78
Kennelly, Colm, 78
Kerr, Frankie, 72f., 88
Kildare Street Club, 30
King James VI Golf Club, Perth, 49
King, J.D., Philadelphian cricketer, 15
Kings Hospital School, 35
Kingstown School, 17, 35
Knights of the Campanile
  accommodation, 81
  functions, 71 et seq.
  fund-raising, 100
  lacrosse matches, 70
  silent tribute by, to florist, 72
  tie, 71
Kyle, Maeve, 84

LACROSSE CLUB, 70
lacrosse in Ireland, 70
LADIES' ATHLETIC CLUB (1947), 84f.
LADIES' BOAT CLUB, 105
LADIES' HOCKEY CLUB
  formed, 68
  representation of, on DUCAC, 69
LADIES' SWIMMING CLUB, 70, 73
Lady Elizabeth Boat Club, 69 et seq.
Lansdowne Football Club, 31, 39f., 44
La Touche, J. J. Digges, 30
Latta, Charlie, 106
Lavan, Joyce, 73f.
LAWN TENNIS CLUB, 48
Lawrence's Handbook of Cricket in
  Ireland, 13, 31, 33 et seq., 36, 54, 120
Leahy, Major M.P., 86, 117 et seq.
Leander Club, 118
Leinster Cricket Club, 35
Leinster Senior Cup (rugby), 44, 56, 74, 106
Lever, Charles, 7
levy, sports, 59, 62 et seq., 78 et seq., 80 et seq.
Limerick University, 102
Lincoln Ramblers, 110
Luce, Arthur Aston, FTCD, 15f., 80, 97
Luce, John Victor, FTCD, 80, 89, 95, 97, 99
Luce Hall, 97, 98 et seq., 108
Lunde, Tjerund, 76
Lyburn, E.F. St J.('Toller'), 87
Lyons, Provost Leland, 88
Lysaght, Edward, 23 et seq.

McAuley, Terry, 96, 107
McCarthy, St George, 56
McCombe, Billy, 107
McConnell, A.J., Provost, 95
McDonald, Alastair, 96
McDonogh, J.A., 68
Mackenzie, D. St Clair, 65
McLoughlin, M.E., 48 et seq.
MacNaughton, Paul, 92
MacNeill, Hugo, 106 et seq.
McNicol, Jane, 93
McQuaid, John Charles, 83
McVeagh, George, 68, 88
Maguire, Tom, 88
Mahaffy, John Pentland, FTCD, 14 and f.,
  15 et seq., 110
Mahon, J.R., 77
Mahony, Noel C., 85, 88
Malan, D.J., 64
Marais, Ivan, 64
Marlborough College, 23
Marlborough, Duke of, 41
Marsh, Provost Narcissus, 6
Martin, B.R., 114
Matthews, Winifred, 90
Meates, Roly, 88
Mecredy, R.J., 46 et seq., 56 et seq.

Meenan, Patrick, 101
Melbourne Cricket Club, 23f.
Meldon, G.J., 43
Meldon, J.M., 17
Meldon, Philip, 43
Mellon, Gordon, 114
Merrion Cricket Club, 35
Metropolitan Hurling Club, 55
Metropolitan Regatta, 105
Millar, Ivan, 87
Miller, R.D.W., 92
Millin, Terence, 67
Milling, Hugh, 104
Mills, Kingston, 92
Mooney, David, 88
Moore, P.C., 76
Moran, Jim, 76
Moran, Kevin, 104
Moran, Patricia, 93
Mornington, Earl of, 13f.
Morphy, G.N., 46
Mostert, C.G. van R., 86
MOTOR CYCLE AND LIGHT
   CAR CLUB, 69
Mullin, Brendan, 106 et seq.
Munn, Lionel, 49, 77
murder, in Rubrics, 8
Museum Building, 10
Museum Players, 110

national anthem, 68
National Athletics and Cycling
   Association of Ireland, 75 et seq.
Neptune Rowing Club, 20
Neville, W.C., 32, 44
Newman, Simon, 90, 99
New Zealand Maoris, 44
NIHE, Dublin, 102
NIHE, Limerick, 102
Norelands, Co. Kilkenny, 13
Northern Football Union, 31
Northern Ireland Amateur
   Athletics Association, 75 et seq.
Northern Ireland Women's
   Amateur Athletics Association, 83
North of Ireland Cricket Club, 70
North of Ireland Football Club, 31

O'Connor, H.S., 86
O'Driscoll, Dr Timothy J., 109f.
O'Grady, Joanne, 106
O'Sullivan, P.J., 113
Oliver, Raymond, 72
Olympic Games
   of 1896, 75 and f.
   London (1948), 83
   Melbourne, Tokyo and Rome, 84
   Moscow (1980), 92
   Antwerp (1920), 100
O'Neill, Tony, 102

ORIENTEERING CLUB, 98
Orr, Philip, 106
Oxford and Cambridge Golfing Society, 69
Oxford University
   first boat race with Cambridge, 2
   first cricket match with Cambridge, 2
   rugby fixtures with, 44

Palmer, A., FTCD, 25
Parke, J.C.
   athlete, 45 et seq.
   captain, Ireland XV, 44
   rugby centre, 45
   tennis player, 48
Parnell, Charles Stewart, 53, 56 and f.
Pavilion, College Park, 1, 38, 50 et sqq., 100
   atmosphere of, 108
   financed by College Races, 38
   construction proposed, 50
      authorized, 51
   deficit, 93
   evil of consumption of drink in, 52
   extended, 63, 81
   in First World War, 59, 61
   permanent bar set up in, 88 et seq.
   refurbishment of (1989-90), 108
   reorganization of bar in, 95 et seq.
Pavilion Members
   membership scheme, 61
   design for tie, 65
peacocks, on College Park, 86
Peel, Sir Robert, 22
Pembroke Club, 18
Pembroke Rowing Club, 18
Phoenix Cricket Club, 13
physical education, 108
Pierse, Arthur, 77
Pike brothers, 65
Pilkington, Clarissa, 88
pink, as university colour
   approved, 67 et seq.
   discontinued for five years, 71
   awards of, to women, 72 et seq.
   racing colour of foundress, 67f.
   revived on new basis, 72 et seq.
Plunket, David, 42
Plunkett, Horace, 53
Polin, R.K.M., 77
Porter, A.M., 48
Portmarnock Golf Club, 49
Portora Royal School, 24, 31, 47
POTHOLING CLUB, 98
'Prancer', the, 7
Pratt, Donald, 88
Prior, John, 104 et seq.
Prole, Robert, 91
public schools
   Dickensian characteristics of, 12
   in England, Trinity men from, 12

influence of, in Ireland, 12
development of sports and sports clubs in, 8
Purcell, N.M., 99

Queen's College, Belfast, 44
Queen's College, Cork, 44
Queen's University, Belfast, 96, 102, 104
Quinlan, Francis, 76
Quinn, J.P., 44

rackets, 9
railways, influence of, 12
Read, H.M., 3, 43, 45
real tennis, 6, 7
record, world, first recognized, 46f.
Rice, A.L.G., 85
riding, 7, 8
RIDING CLUB, 98
RIFLE CLUB, 84 et seq.
rioting, student, 8, 41, 115
road bowling, 8
Robbie, John, 106
Rooke, C.V., 45
Rossall School, 23, 35
Ross, Sir John, 35f.
ROWING CLUB, 18 et sqq.
Rowland, Samuel, 33
Royal Dublin Golf Club, 49
Royal Dublin Society, 81
Royal Irish Yacht Club, 92
Royal Military Academy, Woolwich, 37
Royal St George Yacht Club
origin of, 20f.
Sailing Club's links with, 20f., 92
Royal Schools, 24 and f., 31
Rugby School, 4, 23, 26, 28
Russell, Frank, 114
Rutherfoord, H.E., 48
Ryan, W.J.L., FTCD, 96

SAILING CLUB
achievements, 92
gift to, from Annheuser-Busch Inc., 92
St Andrew's Church, Dublin
built on bowling green, 6
St Andrew's University, 77
St Columba's College, 4, 16, 24 et seq.
St Patrick's College, Maynooth, 102
St Patrick's Well, 7
Samuels, Arthur, 17
Sang, P.W., 86
Santry sports grounds
all-weather hockey pitch at, 90
maintenance of, 82
purchased, 81
pavilion at, 81
extended, 93
Scott, Tallon & Walker, architects, 96
Scriven, George, 32, 44

Shankey, Maeve, 84
Shaw, Capt. J.H., 64, 69, 77, 89
Shillington, Colin, 76, 84
Sigerson, Dr George, 113
Smith, T.H., 23f.
Solomons, Bethel, 45
Solomons, Edwin, 87
South African students, 64 et seq., 74, 86
Sparshott, Tony, 76
sporting commons, 106
sports hall
need for, 93
planning and construction of, 96 et seq.
opened as Luce Hall, 97
Springboks (1969), 91
Spring, Dick, 107f.
Spring, Dónal, 107
SQUASH CLUB, 70
Stack, G.H., 44
Stade Français, 44
Stephenson, George, 106
Stoics XI, 110
Stoker, Abraham, 30, 117
SUB-AQUA CLUB, 100
Sugden, Mark, 44, 65
Sweeney, Jack, 76
SWIMMING CLUB, 47, 99 et seq.
Swords, Co. Dublin, football match at, 22

TABLE TENNIS CLUB, 90, 99
Tamplin, Robin, 88
Taylor, Mrs Joan, 95
Taylor, T.R.B., 72
tennis, and see real tennis
courts, 59, 100 et seq.
TCD Association, 65
Thingmote, 7
Thomond College, Limerick, 102
Thompson, J.K.S., 44
Thornton, E.H., 89, 90
Thrift, H., FTCD, 44 et sqq., 59, 60 and f.,
69, 70, 74, 79
Thrift, W.E., FTCD, 59, 60 and f., 62,
70, 79, 84, 99
Tiedt, Fred, 88
Tom Brown's Schooldays, 23, 25
Towers, William G., DUBC captain, 21, 118
Traill, Anthony, FTCD,
and Athletic Club funds, 51
and Rifle Club, 84
as cricketer, 110
chairman, DUGS, 69
and Pavilion, 63
determined and resourceful tribune, 9
as golfer, 49
president, LACROSSE CLUB, 70
role of, in Trinity sport, 14
Traill, William, 19
Trinity Ball, 63, 82 et seq., 94 et seq.

Trinity College, Dublin
  Board minutes of
    uncomplimentary references in, 2
  Catholics in, 8, 73, 80, 93 *et seq.*
  composition of, 8, 80, 93 *et seq.*
  early games in, 6, 8
  facilities, sports, 1
  formerly a bastion of unionism, 8
  founded, 5
  golden age of, 12
  government of, 6, 94
  history, 5
  image of, presented by sports clubs, 111
  library, 1
    athletics collections of, 2 *et seq.*
  proposed merger of, with UCD, 80f.
  rebuilding schemes, 94 *et seq.*
  referendum among student body of, 97
  relationship of
    with Free State, 64, 68
    with UCD, 73 *et seq.*, 80f.
  South African students at, 64 *et seq.*
  sports hall, 1
  Students' Union, 97
  women admitted to, 8
Trinity Hall, 68, 81, 95
Trinity Trust, 81, 90, 96
Trinity Week, 63 *et seq.*, 82, 94
Trumper, Victor, 43
Tuohy, Liam, 88
Tyrrell, Air Vice-Marshal Sir William, 74

Ulster Defence Association, 92f.
Ulysses, 54, 60f., 113
University College, Cork, 102
university colours, 67
University College, Dublin, 102
University College, Galway, 102
University of Toronto Athletic
  Association, 2
University of Ulster, 102, 104
University Philosophical Society, 65

Usher, Frank, 117

van Druten, Jan, 64 *et seq.*
van Hoey Smith, Lesley, 106
Vincent's Club, 71
virgins, female, 72f.

Walkington, D.B., 45
Wall, Rev. F.H., 26 *et seq.*
Wall, R.M., 26
Walsh, J.M., 95
Wanderers Football Club, 24, 31
Warke, L., 85
Watson, Caroline, 106
Watson, E.J. McCartney
  biography, 3
  papers of, in TCD library, 3
  letters quoted, 25 *et sqq.*
Watterson, John, 106
Watts, W.A., Provost, 92, 100
Well, *see* St Patrick's Well
Wellington, Duke of, 13
West, Charles Burton, 25
West Indies, cricket match with, 68
Westminster School, 23
West, Timothy Trevor, FTCD,
  93, 95 *et seq.*, 99
White, Cyril, 76
Wickham, Terry, 92
Wilde, Oscar
  views of, on cricketers' postures, 12
Wilkins, David, 92
Wilkinson, David, 92
women's clubs
  representation on DUCAC, 69, 71
  WOMEN'S CRICKET CLUB, 43f.
Woods, Stanley, 69
wrestling, 8
Wylie, W.E., 113

Yeats, W.B., 53
Young, Arthur, 33